# Constables, Marshals, and More

**Forgotten Offices in Texas Law Enforcement**

# Constables, Marshals, and More

Forgotten Offices in Texas Law Enforcement

Lorie Rubenser

and

Gloria Priddy

Number 7 in the North Texas Crime and Criminal Justice Series

University of North Texas Press

Denton, Texas

©2011 Lorie Rubenser and Gloria Priddy
All rights reserved.
Printed in the United States of America.

10 9 8 7 6 5 4 3 2 1

Permissions:
University of North Texas Press
1155 Union Circle #311336
Denton, TX 76203-5017

The paper used in this book meets the minimum requirements of the American National Standard for Permanence of Paper for Printed Library Materials, z39.48.1984. Binding materials have been chosen for durability.

Library of Congress Cataloging-in-Publication Data

Rubenser, Lorie, 1970–
 Constables, marshals, and more : forgotten offices in Texas law enforcement / Lorie Rubenser and Gloria Priddy. — 1st ed.
   p. cm. — (Number 7 in the North Texas crime and criminal justice series)
 Includes bibliographical references and index.
 ISBN 978-1-57441-321-2 (cloth : alk. paper) — ISBN 978-1-57441-327-4 (pbk. : alk. paper)
 1. Peace officers—Texas. 2. Law enforcement—Vocational guidance—Texas. I. Priddy, Gloria, 1953- II. Title. III. Series: North Texas crime and criminal justice series ; no. 7.
   HV8145.T4R83 2011
   363.28'209764—dc23
   2011020830

*Constables, Marshals, and More: Forgotten Offices in Texas Law Enforcement* is Number 7 in the North Texas Crime and Criminal Justice Series.

# Dedication

To the men in my family who do this work: my husband, father-in-law, cousin, and grandfather. A group of better men could not be found and I am blessed to have them in my life.
—L.R.

I dedicate this book to my Great Grandfather, Thomas Jefferson Priddy, the First Texas Ranger in Priddy, Texas. He fought Indians in Goldthwaite, Texas, to recover a young girl whom the Indians had kidnapped.

Thomas Jefferson Priddy, Second Company of Texas Rangers (Ranger Muster Roll, Goldthwaite, Texas 1865).
—G.P.

# Contents

Acknowledgments . . . . . . . . . . . . . . . . . . . . . . . . . . . viii

**Chapter 1:** Introduction . . . . . . . . . . . . . . . . . . . . . . . 1

**Chapter 2:** Becoming a Texas Peace Officer . . . . . . . . . . . . . . . . . . 11

**Chapter 3:** Legal Issues . . . . . . . . . . . . . . . . . . . . . . . .17

**Chapter 4:** Constables . . . . . . . . . . . . . . . . . . . . . . . .29

**Chapter 5:** Railroad Police . . . . . . . . . . . . . . . . . . . . . . .47

**Chapter 6:** Racing Commission . . . . . . . . . . . . . . . . . . . . .59

**Chapter 7:** Cattle Brand Inspectors . . . . . . . . . . . . . . . . . . .71

**Chapter 8:** University Police . . . . . . . . . . . . . . . . . . . . . .81

**Chapter 9:** Fire Marshal . . . . . . . . . . . . . . . . . . . . . . . .95

**Chapter 10:** City Marshal . . . . . . . . . . . . . . . . . . . . . . . 103

**Chapter 11:** Texas Alcoholic Beverage Commission . . . . . . . . . . . . 111

**Chapter 12:** Bailiffs . . . . . . . . . . . . . . . . . . . . . . . . . 123

**Chapter 13:** Game Wardens . . . . . . . . . . . . . . . . . . . . . . 131

**Chapter 14:** District Attorney/County Attorney Investigators . . . . . . 139

**Chapter 15:** Conclusion . . . . . . . . . . . . . . . . . . . . . . . . 147

Endnotes . . . . . . . . . . . . . . . . . . . . . . . . . . . . . . . 149

Bibliography . . . . . . . . . . . . . . . . . . . . . . . . . . . . . 175

Index . . . . . . . . . . . . . . . . . . . . . . . . . . . . . . . . 180

# Acknowledgments

We really want to thank all the officers who took their time in helping us with this book. We could not have completed this project without your help. Your insights into the profession bring the chapters to life.

We would also like to thank our publisher, Ron Chrisman. You have been so amazing to work with.

The people we work with everyday are also to be thanked. You let us bounce ideas, take time off, and you lent us your support. To be surrounded by such people in our everyday work-life is truly a blessing.

And finally, we owe a debt of gratitude to our families and our friends for putting up with us during this process. We hope this book makes you proud.

# Chapter 1
# Introduction

Ask people to describe what they think of when someone mentions police and the answer will be remarkably similar from one person to another. Largely, people will picture a white male who works for a city police department and drives quickly through the city in a marked patrol car.[1] Occasionally, a picture of a state trooper or sheriff's deputy will emerge.

Most textbooks dealing with policing in general, or in a specific place in America, also deal only with the three basic types of police: municipal, sheriffs and state police. Federal law enforcement may also receive some level of attention. Entire chapters of policing books are devoted to special units and functions. Even a thorough review may lead the student to feel that their future in policing will take place in only these areas. Where a position such as constable appears, often there is only a line or two of information provided, hardly enough information to indicate the position is of any importance. Criminal Justice students will not seek jobs they do not know about and perhaps some will even turn away from policing because they are not aware of jobs that would suit them.

Much of the problem of coverage for various law enforcement positions relates to the big city focus of research. Very few researchers spend time exploring small or rural policing agencies. The reasons for this focus are obvious. Most researchers are from universities or the federal government. Geographically, they are more likely to be located in urban areas near the large police departments. Additionally, large municipal departments offer a greater variety of subjects to study. Large departments have more personnel, more contacts with the public, and more organizational units: three common areas of study.[2]

Research on a large sample is traditionally considered more reliable and valid. It is more easily generalizable to other populations.[3] It is therefore only natural to see researchers focus on large departments and ignore smaller departments that would not offer them the variety of subjects or the numbers needed.

The public also focuses on large municipal departments, largely due to the attention given them by the media. While corruption and other scandals can and do occur in all types and sizes of law enforcement departments, larger-scale corruption scandals and sensational crimes tend to be located in large departments. These stories are popular media fodder, following the "if it bleeds it leads" idea for choosing stories.[4] OJ Simpson and Rodney King focused the attention of the country, and indeed the world, on Los Angeles. The controversial shooting of a groom on his wedding day focused attention on New York City.[5] Large-scale drug seizures or activities relating to terrorism also seem to center on large departments or federal agencies, particularly those within the Department of Homeland Security.

An additional problem contributes to the narrow focus of research on policing. A variety of state level agencies exist that are so specialized in function as to be routinely ignored by researchers. Most of these agencies are small and have a limited scope of operation, thus not generating large numbers or variety of subjects so greatly desired in quality research. The Texas Racing Commission is one example of such an agency, with only seven law enforcement officers.[6]

## The State of Texas

Texas is the second largest state in the United States, covering a land mass of 261,797.12 square miles and containing a population of 24,326,974 persons.[7] Two hundred fifty-four counties of both rural and urban types subdivide the state. Houston is the largest city in Texas and ranks fourth in size in the US.[8]

The state also displays one of the largest varieties of law enforcement agencies in the United States. Over two-thirds of the law enforcement in Texas operates at the municipal or county level.[9] Departments range in size from the 3,465 officers working for the Texas Department of Public Safety[10] down to agencies of one officer like the constable's office in Crosby County.[11] Each department, large or small, contributes something important to the law enforcement picture of Texas.

## History of Texas Law Enforcement

### Constitutional Roots:

There have been five constitutions in Texas while under U.S. control, and four while Texas was independent or a possession of Mexico or Spain.[12] The first Constitution in Texas under U.S. control took effect in 1845 when Texas became a state. Subsequent versions took effect in 1861 when Texas joined the Confederacy and in 1866 and 1869 during Reconstruction. The 1876 constitution remains active currently and employs a 17-article Bill of Rights and a variety of Amendments to stay current. Each constitution held provisions for law enforcement.[13] The position of constable, for instance, received specific mention in each one.[14]

### The First Police:

Issues of law enforcement first came to Texas in 1823 when Stephen F. Austin created a cadre of 10 rangers whom he charged with protecting his new colony.[15] These men and their work evolved into the modern Texas Rangers. Even though Texas Rangers were essentially a military force for some years during Texas Independence, they commonly receive credit as the first state policing agency in the US.

Positions such as sheriff or constable came to Texas in the early years as general law enforcement needs emerged with the spread of the population. Municipal police in towns and cities across Texas emerged in the middle of the 1800s with Houston establishing its city policing in 1849.[16] Other positions such as railroad police or Racing Commission officers emerged later and in response to very specific needs.

### The Scope of Crime in Texas:

The volume of special needs in a state the size of Texas has created a unique variety of law enforcement positions not found in every state. As with all states, need for policing, either general or specific, relates to crime types and levels. All the crimes existing elsewhere also exist in Texas. Additionally, a variety of border-related crimes involving drugs, illegal aliens, and violence occur in Texas.

Since 1976, the Texas Department of Public Safety has gathered crime statistics from all policing agencies in the state on a monthly basis. All law enforcement agencies in the state of Texas must report statistics on crime in their jurisdiction in a standardized format. These crime statistics form a crime index whereby measurement of crime trends, safety issues, and law enforcement needs becomes possible.[17]

The Texas Department of Public Safety forwards the crime statistics to the FBI for their national data collection efforts, culminating in the Uniform Crime Reports (UCR). From this data, the FBI publishes a crime index. Both the Texas version and the FBI version of the UCR use a set of eight crimes for the Part 1 Offenses or Index Crimes. These offenses include murder, forcible rape, robbery, aggravated assault, burglary, larceny-theft, motor vehicle theft, and arson. The Index Crimes represent the most serious criminal behaviors. By gathering data on these crimes on a statewide and nationwide basis, comparison between locations is possible.[18] Other, less serious offenses, create the Part 2 Offense listing.

Data from the Texas UCR indicates that in 2009, law enforcement officers made 1,205,202 arrests. Drug offenses represent the most common reason for arrest, with 149,789 arrests. Public drunkenness represents the next most common reason for arrest with 142,631 arrests. Larceny-theft represents the most common Index Crime. Law enforcement officers arrested 120,068 persons for this crime in 2009. Murder resulted in 837 arrests in 2009.[19] It should make readers feel safer knowing that the most serious crimes are also the least common.

Drug, gambling, prostitution, and liquor offenses are some of the most common in Texas. These so called "vice" crimes represent a large portion of the work a law enforcement officer will engage in. These crimes also demonstrate the need for specialized law enforcement agencies in Texas.

## Modern Texas Law Enforcement

Jurisdiction is the geographic or subject area assigned to an official. For a police officer, jurisdiction can be both geographic, as in countywide, or subject area-specific as in drug-related crimes.[20] As in other states, in Texas there are four general levels of law enforcement and associated jurisdiction: federal, state, county, and local/municipal. Each level handles a certain set of crimes and within a certain jurisdiction or geographical area.

Federal law enforcement has the largest jurisdiction in terms of geographical area, but is perhaps the most limited on the types of crimes they have authority to handle. Each federal law enforcement agency receives authorization through Congress to deal with specific crimes or situations. With few exceptions, only violations of federal law or offenses that cross state or national boundaries come under the jurisdiction of federal law enforcement.[21]

The most visible federal agencies in Texas now revolve around Homeland Security. US Customs and Border Protection (CBP) combines Immigration, Customs, and Border Patrol and has a particularly high level of visibility in West Texas along the US-Mexico border. The agency is responsible for regulation of cross-border traffic of people and goods. As with all federal agencies, CBP does not usually engage in policing activities such as traffic stops. Exceptions may exist, but the average citizen will normally only deal with CBP when passing through a border area checkpoint.[22]

In addition to federal agencies, Texas has a variety of state-level policing agencies. State level agencies typically operate anywhere within the boundaries of the state. The most well-known state law enforcement agency is the Department of Public Safety. Within this department are both Troopers and Texas Rangers. Troopers are the uniformed patrol officers who commonly interact with motorists on the state's highways. Rangers are plain-clothes investigative officers. Troopers do not normally patrol within the incorporated city limits, but due to their statewide jurisdiction, they can exercise that option. Rangers investigate crimes anywhere in the state.[23]

Other state-level policing agencies in Texas focus on specific areas of law enforcement. The Texas Alcoholic Beverage Commission, for instance, focuses only on crimes and regulatory violations relating to alcohol. These specialized, or limited purpose, agencies normally operate on a statewide basis but within the narrow scope of subjects assigned to them. They do not normally engage in routine policing such as writing speeding tickets.[24]

At the county level, most law enforcement positions are political in nature. A sheriff or constable requires election by voters in order to achieve the position. Most sheriffs' offices engage in regular policing and maintain the county jail. Other county level officers, like the constable, may engage mostly in duties for the courts with regular policing a secondary function.[25] Although an incorporated area of a city occupies a geographic area within a county, normally county level officers like sheriffs do not engage in routine police work within these areas unless requested to do so.

The vast majority of policing everywhere in the US is accomplished through local, municipal policing agencies. These officers' jurisdictions are limited geographically to the city limits. Of all the levels of law enforcement in the state, municipal police have the widest range of crimes in their jurisdiction. Municipal police also hold the most responsibility for order maintenance and community service activities.[26]

The combined efforts of officers at all four levels of law enforcement provide Texans with protection from things ranging from the criminal to the annoying. They accomplish this through activities ranging from random patrol to crime investigations and prevention efforts.

According to Lillian Alderete of the Texas Commission on Law Enforcement Officer Standards and Education, in the state of Texas 68,410 persons hold licenses as Texas Peace Officers. Many of these persons hold a commission with more than one agency. Of this total, 39,878 work for municipal departments, 31,701 for sheriff's offices,[27] and 3,465 for the Texas Department of Public Safety.[28] An additional 13,178 persons are licensed peace officers but do not work for these agencies.[29] One may ask what role these other 13,178 officers play in Texas law enforcement.

The state of Texas displays a wide variety of specialized policing positions, many of which exist in other states: constables and university/campus police for example. Some of these positions, such as cattle brand inspectors, may be unique to Texas or a few select other states.

Along with the great variation in policing positions in Texas, great variation exists within positions. A constable in East Texas around the Dallas/Ft. Worth metroplex will be paid differently and do a completely different job than a constable in rural West Texas. Similar differences between urban and rural officers occur within any law enforcement position in Texas.

## Overview of the Book

All law enforcement officers in the state of Texas begin their careers in a similar fashion. Regardless of the position, each officer has met the same basic entry criteria and must abide by the same legal foundations. Our discussion must therefore begin with the basics and then move into the specialized areas of Texas law enforcement.

Chapter 2 explains the process whereby an interested individual would become a Texas peace officer. The chapter begins with the criteria for initial consideration and moves through the hiring process. It concludes with information on the requirements for maintaining an active peace officer license throughout a career.

Chapter 3 examines the basic constitutional and statutory foundations of Texas law enforcement. Coverage includes the types of officers who are designated peace officers, their basic responsibilities and duties, their jurisdiction, and some of the limitations on their authority.

The remaining sections of the book focus on expanding the reader's view of law enforcement in Texas. Plenty of books concerning municipal police, sheriffs, and state police exist. The Texas Rangers in particular are the subject of many books and articles. Even police academy training in the state of Texas receives coverage. We have deliberately left those positions out in order to focus on the lesser known but equally important positions that exist in the wide array of Texas law enforcement.

Chapter 4 begins the exploration of the specialized law enforcement positions by describing constables. The chapter begins with a historical overview of constables and progresses through the modern position and its specialized requirements. It concludes with a discussion of the actual day-to-day activities of modern constables in the state of Texas.

Some of the most specialized positions in Texas law enforcement appear in chapters 5–7: railroad police, Texas Racing Commission officers, and cattle brand inspectors, for instance. Each agency is small in scope but they represent some of the most important law enforcement functions in the state when considered in terms of their impact on the state's development. By ensuring safe transport of persons and cargo, fair sporting practices, and upholding property rights of ranchers, these officers have contributed to the livelihood of Texas citizens and to the state's economy in ways that cannot be overestimated. Each chapter will demonstrate the impact of these small but important agencies both in law enforcement and in the overall picture of the state of Texas.

Many readers are probably familiar with university police at a basic level. College students often interact with university police over parking tickets, troubles in dormitories, and petty thefts. This is, however, only the beginning of the responsibilities assigned to university police departments. Many universities assign fire protection, risk management, issuance of campus ID cards and keys, and other tasks not traditionally thought of as police work to their campus police departments. University police are also under increasing scrutiny concerning their ability to maintain campus safety due to the shootings at Virginia Tech in 2008 and Northern Illinois University in 2009. Chapter 8 will explore university police and this wide variety of tasks assigned to them, demonstrating just how complex this job really is.

Another Texas law enforcement position that is relatively unknown is the fire marshal. While most people probably think of fire marshals as persons who check fire alarms and investigate arsons, many do not know that fire marshals are also law enforcement officers with all the normal policing powers. Chapter 9 explores this position and demonstrates how law enforcement powers are essential to the work of the fire marshal.

City marshals are the subject of chapter 10. City marshals used to be the only law enforcement in some cities, especially in the West. Today, their main duty is to serve warrants for the courts. Many times these warrants are for failure to appear in court as scheduled. The city marshal will often issue persons subject to such warrants a personal recognizance bond so that the person will have the chance to go to the court and explain their circumstances and pay their fines. The chapter shows both the rich western history of the city marshal as well as the still thriving position as it exists today.

Chapter 11 focuses on the Texas Alcoholic Beverage Commission (TABC). Officers in this organization are responsible for regulating all things related to alcohol in the state of Texas including licensing and sales. The public generally only sees these agents when they are on the news conducting sting operations to stop the sale of alcohol to minors. The result is generally a negative view. Chapter 11 will show the variety of prevention efforts and other duties TABC officers are responsible for and demonstrate how the seemingly predatory sting operations are only a minor portion of the TABC officer's work.

The position of bailiff is an up and coming specialized law enforcement position. These officers work in both county and district courts to provide security for court personnel and persons attending court. Their presence helps keep order and ensure a smoothly flowing court process. Chapter 12 will trace the history of this position and show how far beyond being a bodyguard for the judge the position has moved.

Achieving a position as Game Warden is a common goal among criminal justice students. Many, however, do not understand the full scope of this position. Game Wardens cover camping, hunting regulations, and water safety on public lands and waterways. The focus is on preservation of Texas wildlife and the environment. Chapter 13 will discuss this position in detail to demonstrate how these officers not only enforce the law but also protect Texas' vast array of natural resources and wildlife for present and future generations.

The final chapter on a specialized law enforcement position is devoted to peace officers who serve as investigators for District Attorney and County Attorney offices. The investigator position is important as successful prosecution of criminal cases often depends as much on the work of the investigator as it does on the prosecutor.

The conclusion to the book will wrap up the discussions of the various special positions in Texas law enforcement. An overall picture of the wide variety of policing in Texas appears here, thus demonstrating that not all police jobs are equal. Nor do they all exist in city departments, sheriff's offices or with the state police.

# Chapter 2

# Becoming a Texas Peace Officer

Although great variety exists in Texas law enforcement positions and duties, every peace officer in the state, regardless of position, must meet the same initial requirements. Each officer starts out on the same basic footing and then begins their unique adventure in the world of law enforcement.

## Qualifying as a Peace Officer in the State of Texas

In the state of Texas, all peace officers and reserves must hold a license through the Texas Commission on Law Enforcement Officer Standards and Education (TCLEOSE). Created by the 59th Texas Legislature on September 1, 1965, TCLEOSE ensures peace officers across the state of Texas are able to meet the demands of a law enforcement career.[1]

Beyond just issuing licenses to peace officers, TCLEOSE now sets eligibility standards, develops training curriculum for academies and continuing education providers, and enforces standards for peace officers, academies, and other associated professionals. TCLEOSE also processes license revocations and training and employment records.[2]

Currently TCLEOSE deals with 2,653 agencies spread over seven regions across Texas. This includes 300 training providers who run academies or provide continuing education programs.[3] Rules set by TCLEOSE for academy training include rules on who may receive the training. The eligibility standards peace officer candidates must meet include the following criteria:

- Possession of a high school diploma, GED, or 12 hours of college credit,
- Being at least 21 years old or at least 18 and possessing an Associate degree, 60 hours of college credit or an honorable discharge from the military after at least 2 years of active service,
- Possession of a clean criminal record with no convictions for offenses above a Class B misdemeanor (five- and ten-year time limits may apply to those with a Class B misdemeanor),
- Having no pending indictments and no family violence offense convictions of any kind,
- Having no prohibitions against motor vehicle operation or firearms possession,
- Passing a background check, physical examination, psychological examination, and drug screening,
- If former military, possession of an honorable discharge,
- Having not had a peace officer license that was denied, suspended or revoked,
- Having not violated TCLEOSE rules or the provisions of Chapter 1701 of the Occupations Code,
- Possession of US citizenship,
- Having met the minimum training requirements and passing the licensing exam.[4]

Before taking the licensing exam, candidates who have met the criteria listed above must attend a period of law enforcement training or a basic peace officer academy. Academy criteria and curriculum regulation occurs through TCLEOSE. Current academy requirements include 618 hours of training in various academic and practical application subjects. Texas law, specialty areas of police duty such as dealing with victims and report writing, Spanish for law enforcement, and other academic subject areas are covered. Practical application areas include self-defense, driving, and firearms. Upon successful completion of an academy, persons may take the licensing exam, a 200-question multiple-choice test administered by TCLEOSE. Anyone scoring 70 percent or higher on the licensing exam is issued a peace officer license and may then seek employment as a law enforcement officer.[5]

## The Hiring Process

The law enforcement academy at Sul Ross State University is a regional academy that runs basic peace officer training over 18 weeks. Cadets pay $1,500 to attend this academy. Cost covers uniforms, ammunition, and other supplies.[6]

Whereas regional academies require cadets to pay for their training, in-house academies operated by specific police departments typically provide a salary for their cadets, with the understanding that the cadets will then work for the specific departments after academy graduation. The Dallas Police Department is an example of an in-house academy system. Cadets are paid $42,690 as a beginning salary with pay starting after completion of the first two weeks of academy training.[7]

Each department across the state will conduct officer hiring according to its own standards. Some departments will hire only persons who already hold licenses as peace officers. Others will not require a license as they send all persons through an in-house academy to achieve licensing. Each department chooses its own procedures; however, the process normally begins with a lengthy application detailing employment history, education, criminal record, and other relevant details.[8]

Most departments will conduct a thorough background check of any applicant to determine character, maturity level, integrity, and other personal characteristics. A criminal record check is normally part of this process.[9] Driving and credit histories may also be checked. The written application serves as a beginning point for the investigation. Any gaps in the information provided on the application make the process more difficult and may lead to rejection.[10] Additionally, for applicants who had previous employment in law enforcement, TCLEOSE is now requiring contact with each previous employer prior to hiring an officer.[11]

If an applicant remains eligible based on the application and background check, they can expect to face several other steps before being hired. A written examination is a common practice. The examination assesses reading comprehension and writing skills as well as vocabulary and general knowledge.[12] The test complies with state civil service regulations in order to ensure a fair opportunity to all applicants.[13]

An oral interview with one or more officers and sometimes an interview with a board of officers are also common. The interviews assess verbal ability as well as problem-solving skills and ethical standards.[14] Interview boards often have a standardized list of questions that all candidates must answer, which ensure fairness and increase the comparability of answers.[15]

Candidates will also typically take a physical agility test. Testing may include timed tasks, which relate to the performance of the police job, including running, jumping, dead weight carrying, and other physical endurance tests. Tests of this type ensure the potential officer has the ability to meet the basic physical requirements of the job and to ensure that the applicant is healthy enough to take on academy training.[16]

In addition to physical agility tests as a measure of health, many departments will require a medical examination. A drug screening may also be required as part of this procedure or as a procedure of its own.[17] Candidates with health issues may be screened out due to the potential of increased injury, illness, and disability. Candidates with a previous history of drug use may or may not progress in the hiring process, depending on the nature of the previous use. Type of drugs used, amount of use, length of time from last use, etc. help determine continued eligibility. Generally, candidates who are currently using or have a history of heavy drug use/dependency will be screened out.[18]

Applicants may also be subject to a psychological exam. The exam often uses a standardized test such as the Minnesota Multiphasic Personality Inventory (MMPI).[19] Tests of this nature measure aspects of personality such as personal and social adjustment, anxiety, etc. The object is to weed out candidates who have indicators of personality disorders that may inhibit their ability to function under stress or other conditions of the job. Persons with impulse control issues, for instance, may have difficulty functioning in the highly structured environment of the law and its enforcement.[20]

Applicants may also take a polygraph examination, which helps show how truthful the applicant is being while answering a series of questions. Obviously, the more truthful an applicant is the better. Questions during this examination may cover issues about personal life such as drug use and criminal behavior.[21] Lying about these issues may result in rejection even if the issue itself would not.

Departments may also have specific requirements for employment with their agency, or for the particular job the applicant is seeking. Specific requirements may include education levels and skills or training in a specialized area such as computers. Job postings for a given department will normally spell out any unique requirements so only potential candidates who meet these requirements will apply.

An applicant can face elimination from the potential hiring pool at any stage in the process. Upon successful completion of all required steps, the applicant is normally hired either as a recruit who will attend a police academy, or directly as an officer if the applicant is already state certified.[22] The new officer may also be subject to a period of field training where they will work closely with a veteran training officer to learn what being an officer really means in that particular department.[23]

Applicants who meet the basic qualifications and survive the hiring process and academy training are uniquely prepared to enter the world of Texas law enforcement. Over the course of an officer's career, many will move into specialized positions within a department or into a special area of law enforcement like railroad policing. Regardless of where they serve, all officers have met or exceeded the standards of entry into the profession.

## Continuing Education for Peace Officers

Training for Texas peace officers does not end with the academy. In order to maintain a license as a peace officer, state law requires a minimum of 40 hours of continuing education within a two-year training cycle. This requirement comes from TCLEOSE, who may suspend the peace officer license of any person who fails to complete the required training. The 40 hours of required training include Cultural Diversity, Crisis Intervention, and Special Investigative Topics courses. Special Investigative Topics covers the subjects of child abuse/neglect, family violence, sexual assault, and sex offender characteristics.[24]

## Levels of Peace Officer Certification

Once admitted to the profession, officers may achieve additional status in the field by completing the requirements for additional levels of peace officer certification. All licensed peace officers in the state of Texas start out with a Basic Peace Officer certification level. Achievement of advanced certification levels depends on a sliding scale of years of service, TCLEOSE training hours, and college education.[25]

The second level of peace officer certification is the Intermediate Peace Officer and requires a minimum of two years of service and a bachelor's degree or

2400 hours of TCLEOSE training. More years of service are required for those with less college education or fewer training hours. Additionally, officers must complete a series of required training courses including the intermediate levels of Child Abuse Prevention and Investigation, Crime Scene Investigation, Use of Force, and Arrest, Search and Seizure. Spanish for Law Enforcement, Asset Forfeiture, Racial Profiling, Identity Theft, and a choice of Train the Trainer, Crisis Intervention, or Mental Health Peace Officer are also required.[26]

The third level of certification is the Advanced Peace Officer level, requiring the Intermediate Peace Officer certification and a minimum of five years of service with a bachelor's degree or six years of service with 2400 TCLEOSE training hours. Additionally, if the officer did not take the Train the Trainer course already, they must do so at this level.[27]

The fourth and final level of certification is the Master Peace Officer level. At this level, the officer must have met all the requirements of the Advanced Peace Officer level. The officer must also have a minimum of five years of service with a doctoral degree or a maximum of 20 years of service with 1200 hours of TCLEOSE training.[28]

Each of the levels of certification discussed above is available to any officer in the state of Texas. The type of position an officer holds or the agency they work for does not matter, although some agencies will offer pay incentives or other rewards to officers who have achieved higher levels of certification. Some will also base promotions and special assignments in part on an officer's level of certification.

## Conclusion

Law enforcement officers often have the power of life and death, literally, over members of the public. In order to help prepare them for this awesome responsibility, all officers in the state of Texas are required to meet the same entry criteria and are subject to the same basic training requirements. The availability of increasing levels of certification provides motivation and rewards to officers who enhance their skills and knowledge while on the job.

Once a person has met the requirements and become a peace officer, their career begins to take on its own unique characteristics. As unique as their career may be, each officer remains bound by the legal limitation provided by state and federal laws.

# Chapter 3

# Legal Issues

By Special Guest Author Raymond G. Kessler, J.D.

## Introduction

The purpose of this chapter is to provide an overview of the legal bases of authority for Texas police agencies and individual Texas peace officers under Texas law. Although the Texas Constitution says little of relevance, there are thousands of pages of statutes and administrative regulations relevant to peace officers in general, or just to specific types of peace officers. This chapter will thus provide only a summary of the broadest principles, and some selected specific provisions and court decisions.

## Federalism

In the United States, government power is divided between the federal government and state governments—a system referred to as federalism.[1] The Tenth Amendment to the United States Constitution provides that "the powers not delegated to the United States by the Constitution, nor prohibited by it to the states, are reserved to the states respectively..."[2]

Among these reserved powers are the "police power"—a broad-ranging power to regulate for the protection of public health, welfare, safety, and morals.[3] While the federal government has a police power over geographical locations within its control (e.g., military reservations), it has no such general power in locations subject to state jurisdiction (within the states themselves).[4] Thus, all of the states have a reserved power under the US Constitution to legislate to protect the public in that state. That power, of course, includes power to pass criminal laws and enforce those laws by the creation of law enforcement agencies and the grant of authority to law enforcement officers.[5] Thus, state power, including its police power, is derived from and limited by, the constitution of that particular state and the Constitution of the United States.[6] The federal constitutional limitations are widely covered in other sources,[7] and will not be treated here.

## Texas Constitution

The police power of the state is exercised and delegated primarily through the legislature. The police power may also be delegated to counties, municipalities, and other governmental entities to promote the public welfare.[8]

The Texas Constitution[9] has little to say about peace or law enforcement officers. Excluding amendments, it mentions only two types of peace officers—sheriffs and constables. Article 5 sec. 18 provides for the office of constable. Article 5 sec. 23 provides for the office of Sheriff in each county. Neither section specifies the duties or powers of these officers.

Article I of the Texas Constitution is the state Bill of Rights, which limits the powers of state government and law enforcement. It contains many provisions similar to those in the federal Bill of Rights. Unlike the US Constitution's Bill of Rights, the Texas Constitution's Bill of Rights provides rights for crime victims (sec. 30). Victims of crime are entitled to be treated with fairness. Their rights to dignity and their privacy must be respected by law enforcement and other criminal justice personnel. Victims also have a right to reasonable protection from defendants.

## What Texas Officials are Peace Officers?

Background:
A peace officer is an agent of the government, which employs him or her. That officer's power and jurisdiction are derived from both state law and the government entity that employs the officer.[10] Different types of police or peace officers have different types of authority and jurisdiction.[11]

The creation of *state* peace officers and agencies and the grant of their powers is covered primarily by the Texas Government Code.[12] Specialized peace officers are often created and empowered by specific codes in Texas statutes, such as the Education Code.[13] The creation of local peace officers and agencies and their empowerment is covered primarily by the Texas Local Government Code.[14.]

### At Least 35 Types of Peace Officers:

Section 2.01 (a) 36 of the Texas Penal Code[15] adopts, by reference, the definitions of "peace officer" found in Texas Code of Criminal Procedure article 2.12, Education Code sections 51.212, 51.214, and "other law."

Texas Code of Criminal Procedure article 2.12 attempts to collect the scattered laws on types of peace officers and specifies 35 different definitions/categories of peace officer.[16] Some of these, such as sheriffs, constables, city police officers, and Texas Rangers, are well known. Others, such as officers commissioned by the State Board of Dental Examiners and Texas Racing Commission, are less well known. (The relevant sections of the Education Code are discussed later in this chapter.)

The Code of Criminal Procedure also provides for even more specialized peace officers who have significantly limited powers. Examples are "Railroad Peace Officers" (article 2.121), "Special Investigators" (article. 2.122), and "Adjunct Peace Officers" (article. 2.123). There is also a provision, article 2.124, giving peace officers from adjoining states limited authority in Texas. There are additional, obscure officers who may qualify as peace officers to a limited extent.[17]

## Jurisdiction

An officer's powers and duties are limited to the locations that are within the officer's (geographic) jurisdiction within the state.[18] Texas Code of Criminal Procedure article 2.13 provides that a peace officer is to keep the peace "within the officer's jurisdiction." This section does not define that jurisdiction, and one must look to a variety of sometimes ambiguous and conflicting statutes to determine a peace officer's jurisdiction.[19]

Under Texas Government Code, sections 411.022 and 411.032, some peace officers, such as Texas Rangers and Texas Highway Patrol officers, have statewide jurisdiction. Others generally are limited to certain legally defined areas on the state. For instance, under Texas Code of Criminal Procedure, article 2.17, a sheriff generally has jurisdiction only in "his county."

In addition to general jurisdictional statutes, the legislature has passed statutes providing for exceptions to the usual rules in certain circumstances.[20] For instance, under certain circumstances, an officer who is outside his or her jurisdiction may make a warrantless arrest (e.g., Texas Code of Criminal Procedure article 14.03 d).

This is a complex area of law because peace officers' jurisdiction to carry out one kind of duty (e.g., make a warrantless arrest or serve an arrest warrant) is often different from their jurisdiction to perform other tasks.[21] Reamey & Harkins note that there is "significant ambiguity" with regard to peace officer jurisdiction because of "imprecise statutory language, varying judicial interpretations and numerous overlapping, and sometimes conflicting statutes."[22]

## General Duties, Powers, etc. of All Peace Officers

Texas Code of Criminal Procedure article 2.13 provides that it is the duty of all Texas peace officers to "preserve the peace within the officer's jurisdiction." To accomplish these goals, officers are authorized to "use all lawful means." Among the specific means mentioned in this article are interfering without warrants to suppress or prevent crime, execute lawful process, give notice to magistrates of offenses, and arrest, without warrant, when authorized by law.

Summoning Assistance:

Article 2.14 of the Texas Code of Criminal Procedure provides that when a peace officer meets with resistance when discharging his or her legal duties, he or she "shall summon a sufficient number of citizens of his county to overcome the resistance . . ." All persons so summoned are "bound to obey."

Racial Profiling:

Texas Code of Criminal Procedure article 2.131 prohibits racial profiling. Racial profiling is defined by article 3.05 of that Code as any action by law enforcement officers that is based on the person's national origin, ethnicity, or race, rather than on their behavior or on information about the individual. Articles 2.131 through 2.138 of the Texas Code of Criminal Procedure impose specific requirements with regard to racial profiling. Agencies and officers are required to make reports, compile data, adopt policies, etc.

# Chapter 3: Legal Issues

### Licensing, Training, etc:

The Texas Commission Law Enforcement Officer Standards and Education (TCLEOSE) has a number of requirements which apply to peace officers with regard to licensing, training, certification, minimum standards, etc.[23] For instance, peace officers must be at least 21 years of age and must, in general, have graduated from high school or have a GED.[24]

### Statewide Code of Ethics:

TCLEOSE has adopted the International Association of Chiefs of Police Code of Ethics, and requires that it be distributed, read, and discussed in all Basic Peace Officer academies.[25] This code of ethics provides that the fundamental duties of law enforcement are to serve humankind, safeguard life and property, and protect "the innocent against deception, the weak against oppression or intimidation, and the peaceful against violence or disorder; and to respect the Constitutional rights of all men to liberty, equality and justice." The code also requires officers to keep their private lives "unsullied" and be an example to others. Officers are also expected to "maintain courageous calm in the face of danger, scorn, or ridicule, develop self-restraint; and be constantly mindful of the welfare of others." They are directed to preserve confidences, be honest in both deed and thought in both their official and personal lives, and be a positive example in following the law and departmental regulations.[26]

Other ethical imperatives are to avoid unnecessary force and accepting gratuities, acting "officiously" and letting personal attitudes or relationship affect official decisions. Officers are directed to relentlessly pursue criminals and never compromise with crime.[27]

### Missing and Abused Children:

Officers also have a wide variety of duties with regard to missing and abused children. For instance, Texas Code of Criminal Procedure article 2.13 (c) provides that every officer has a duty to take possession of a child covered by Article 63.009(g) of that Code. Article 63.009 (g) deals with duties of law enforcement agencies incumbent upon receiving a report of a missing child or person. In general, law enforcement agencies are required to start investigations, enter information in various clearinghouses or the National Crime Information Center, notify certain persons, and make arrests in certain cases. Additional duties with regard to missing children are imposed on Texas law enforcement agencies by Articles 63.011 through 63.016 of the same Code. Duties with regard to certain child abuse cases are imposed by Code of Criminal Procedure article 2.27. A peace officer from an appropriate law enforcement agency is required to investigate high priority referrals from the Texas Department of Protective and Regulatory Services.

Family Violence Prevention:

Texas Code of Criminal Procedure chapter 5, and Texas Family Code chapter 86[28] detail the obligations of Texas Peace officers with regard to preventing family violence. These include duties with regard to arrest, reports, investigation, data entry, and notices.[29] Article 5.01 (a) of the Code of Criminal Procedure provides that victims of family violence are entitled to the "maximum protection" allowed by law. Article 5.01 (b) of the same Code provides that when law enforcement responds to allegations of family violence, officers must protect the victim "without regard to the relationship between the alleged offender and victim."

According to Texas Code of Criminal Procedure Article 5.04 the primary duties of peace officers investigating family violence are to (1) protect potential victims, (2) enforce state law, (3) enforce protective orders from other jurisdictions and (4) arrest violators. Officers also have a variety of duties with regard to investigations, reports, notifications, arrests, etc. Article 5.045 (a) of the Code of Criminal Procedure provides that officers may, at their discretion, stay with family violence victims while such victims remove their personal property to a place of safety in an orderly manner.

Duties of Peace Officers Regarding Threats:

The Code of Criminal Procedure chapter 6 imposes duties on peace officers to protect citizens against injury threatened by others. This duty may be imposed by a magistrate who has learned of the threat, or when a peace officer personally learns of the threat (articles 6.01–6.07). Under Article 6.05, the officer "may take such measures as the person about to be injured might for the prevention of the offense." Officers may use force, but may not use more force than is necessary (article 6.06). Under article 6.08, officers have duties to protect persons covered by protective orders in cases involving bias or prejudice against victims (hate crimes).

# Chapter 3: Legal Issues

### Contraband Forfeiture:

According to Chapter 59 of the Code of Criminal Procedure, officers and agencies have a number of duties with regard to forfeitable contraband. These include obligations relating to the proceeds from drug sales, property purchased with the proceeds of illegal drug sales, etc. These duties involve, *inter alia*, seizure, notification, care, custody, reports, and disposition.

### Suppressing Riots:

Pursuant to Texas Code of Criminal Procedure chapter 8, peace officers have a duty to disperse those engaged in rioting, unlawful assemblies, or other unlawful disturbances as defined the Texas Penal Code. Code article 8.06 provides that officers may use force, "but are not authorized to use any greater degree of force than is requisite to accomplish that object."

### Alcoholic Beverage Code:

Texas Peace Officers also have certain powers under the Texas Alcoholic Beverage Code.[30] Under Code sec. 101.07, all peace officers are required to enforce this Code and assist the Alcoholic Beverage Commission in detecting offenses and apprehending violators. For instance, under that Code's section 101.02, officers can make warrantless arrests and seizures for violations of the Code or administrative regulations. Section 101.04 of the Code provides that peace officers are not required to obtain a warrant before inspecting or investigating premises covered by a license or permit.

### Texas Transportation Code:

The Texas Transportation Code includes a multitude of rights and duties for peace officers. These include accident investigations and reports, traffic control, and pursuits.[31] Under section 543.001, peace officers may make warrantless arrests for certain traffic violations, and, in general, offenders must "immediately" be taken before a magistrate. In other situations (section 543.0904), the officer "shall" issue a written notice or ticket. There are numerous duties with regard to drunk driving and related cases.[32]

During high-speed pursuits or emergencies, officers have certain obligations with regard to the use of lights, audible signals, etc., as required by sections 546.003, and 546.004. During such emergencies, officers are privileged or authorized by sections 546.001 and 546.002 to violate certain rules of the road such as speed limits, stop signs, etc. However, even in an emergency, officers must still take certain precautions. Under section 546.001 (2), when running a red light or stop sign the officer must slow "as necessary for safe operation." When speeding, the officer, under section 546.001 (3), "must not endanger life or property." In addition, according to section 546.001 (1), the vehicle must be operated "with appropriate regard for the safety of all persons."

Juvenile Offenders:

The Texas Family Code imposes a number of duties on peace officers with regard to juvenile suspects.[33] Under the Family Code there are special rules for arresting (section 52.01) and detaining ( section 52.02) juveniles (as compared to adult offenders). Peace officers who want to take statements from juvenile suspects must follow the strict procedures in Family Code section 51.095.

Drug Laws:

As part of their general obligation to enforce the law and make arrests, Texas peace officers also enforce the state's lengthy and complex drug laws.[34] Texas Health and Safety Code, chapters 481–485 outline the primary duties of peace officers. For instance, peace officers and agencies also have duties with regard to forfeiture and destruction of controlled substance plants (chapter 481, subchapter E,), and certain reports (section. 481.185).

Statements and Confessions:

Under Texas Code of Criminal Procedure article 38.21, statements are admissible only as provided by statute and only if "freely and voluntarily made without compulsion or persuasion." Article 38.22 provides additional rules. Different rules apply depending upon whether the statement is written or oral. These complex requirements go well beyond those required by *Miranda v. Arizona* (1966).[35]

## Selected Arrest, Search, and Seizure Issues

Texas peace officers must meet all the requirements of the Fourth Amendment and Article I section 9 of the Texas Constitution. In addition, numerous Texas statutes regulate such activity. Texas peace officers are also subject to the federal exclusionary rule and the Texas exclusionary rule (Texas Code

# Chapter 3: Legal Issues

of Criminal Procedure Article 38.23).[36] This section will focus only on Texas statutes relevant to common police methods of investigating crime.

## Search Warrants:

Texas Code of Criminal Procedure chapter 18 authorizes peace officers to obtain search warrants. Consistent with the Fourth Amendment,[37] code articles 18.01 b and 18.04 (2), require that search warrants be based on probable cause, be supported by an affidavit, and be specific as to the places to be searched and the things to be seized. Search warrants must be executed before they expire (article 18.07), and, under articles 18.06–18.11, officers have certain responsibilities with regard to execution and return of the warrant.

## Wiretapping and Electronic Eavesdropping:

Pursuant to federal law, Texas is one of 22 states that authorize law enforcement interception of electronic communications in certain forms.[38] Under Texas Code of Criminal Procedure article 18.20, to engage in such interception, a peace officer must submit an application for interception (similar to a search warrant affidavit) to a designated District Court Judge. If approved, except in emergency circumstances, the interception must be controlled by personnel from the Texas Department of Public Safety. Such authorization may be obtained only if there is probable cause to believe that the interception will provide evidence of certain specified types of felonies specified in section 4.

## Stop and Frisk:

There is no statute giving Texas peace officers general authority to engage in stop and frisk tactics. However, Texas Courts have permitted such actions as long as the requirements of the Texas and US Constitutions are satisfied.[39]

## Arrest:

Chapter 15 of the Code of Criminal Procedure authorizes peace officers to obtain arrest warrants. Under Article 15.26, when executing an arrest warrant, "it shall always be made known to the accused under what authority the arrest is made." Article 15.24 provides that when making an arrest, all "reasonable means are permitted, but "[n]o greater force, however, shall be resorted to than is necessary to secure the arrest and detention of the accused."

Code of Criminal Procedure article 15.17 (a), provides that whether the arrest is with or without a warrant, peace officers must take all arrestees before the proper magistrate "without unnecessary delay, but not later than 48 hours" after the arrest. As discussed above, there are special rules covering arrests and processing of juveniles.

Warrantless Arrests:

Texas law on warrantless arrests is stricter than that in some states and under the Fourth Amendment. In Texas, warrantless arrests are illegal unless authorized by statute.[40] Most of the warrantless arrest statutes are in chapter 14 of the Code of Criminal Procedure. Most of these articles make the arrest decision discretionary by using the terminology "may arrest." Only one portion of chapter 14 of that code, Article 14.03 b, provides that the officer "shall" arrest. Arrest is mandatory if the officer has probable cause to believe the person has violated certain protective orders and the offense is committed in the officer's presence.

DWI Checkpoints:

Although the US Supreme Court approved Michigan's DWI checkpoints in the *Sitz* case,[41] the Court of Criminal Appeals has interpreted the Fourth Amendment and *Sitz* to preclude such checkpoints in Texas. This can only be done once such checkpoints are authorized by a statewide policy promulgated by a statewide, politically accountable body.[42] Texas statutes do allow drivers' license checkpoints.[43] However, officers cannot set up drivers' license checkpoints as a subterfuge for DWI enforcement.[44]

## Conclusion

Most Texas peace officers have a very wide set of powers, duties, and obligations. Others have relatively limited powers and jurisdiction. This is a very complex area of the law. The Texas Legislature seems to add to this complexity every legislative session. They do this not only by adding new criminal offenses, but also by creating new duties or authority.[45] They also frequently create new types of peace officers, such as the "Special Rangers of the Texas and Southwestern Cattle Raisers Association," described in Texas Code of Criminal Procedure article 2.125.

The legal bases of the Texas peace officers' authority and obligations are also constantly changing through statutes, administrative regulations, and court decisions, so the reader is advised to check for changes in the material cited above. This chapter has only scratched the surface of this large and difficult area of Texas law.[46]

Constable Alivie Hester, Tom Green County.

*Photo Courtesy of Alivie Hester.*

# Chapter 4

# Constables

## Introduction

Constables are one of the many undervalued and understudied positions in American law enforcement. The position exists in various forms across the United States and in several countries. In England, for example, the constable is a position akin to the metropolitan patrol officer in America. Constables in the United States tend to be more specialized in their role and duties.[1]

As originally conceived, the position of constable was not about law enforcement, but rather it was a servant position in the King's household. The constable oversaw the stables and kennels, and any other matter relating to the sport of hunting.[2] The constable also sat in judgment over many issues such as land ownership, inheritance, chivalry, honor, etc.[3]

The position evolved over time through military responsibilities[4] and tax collection duties[5] into domestic peace keeping.[6] The constable is now an important part of the law enforcement tradition around the world.

## British History of the Position

The position of constable has existed in one form or another as far back as 438 A.D., though not always as a law enforcement position. The name comes from the Latin "comes stubuli" meaning master of the horse. The first recorded appearance of the constable position occurred in the Roman Empire when Emperor Theodosius appointed a man as head of the royal stables.[7]

King Alfred may have established constables in England as early as 871 A.D. The constables' duties included rendering judgment in cases of military offenses, chivalry, and honor.[8] Additionally, the constable was in charge of athletic competitions such as jousting.[9] The position was largely a reflection of the French position of constable.[10]

The position of constable gained further prominence in England following the Norman Conquest in 1066. Persons holding the constable position were responsible for matters relating to the royal militia, including armaments. The position evolved under King Stephen to become Lord High Constable, the King's representative in all military matters.[11]

Constables are mentioned under British law beginning with the Magna Carta in 1215 and continuing through various laws including the Statute of Westminster in 1285 where provisions were created to assign two constables to every hundred (local units of governance created by grouping communities into groups of 100 adult males). The constable was the first form of English police officer. Constables were responsible for dealing with all serious breaches of the law.[12]

When the Black Death came to England, constables were on the front line of combating the spread of the deadly plague. They oversaw the movements of persons, especially workers, from area to area in order to isolate the healthy population from the infected persons.[13]

Through the years, the constable's duties relating to law enforcement or peacekeeping expanded in direct proportion to the expansion of administrative duties for the sheriff.[14] To assist in their peacekeeping mission, constables relied upon night watchmen in the various communities. Twice a year the constable would inspect the night watchmen and see to their armament.[15]

## American History of the Position

Constables have existed in America as far back as colonial times. In 1632, Plymouth Colony appointed its first constable.[16] Under the supervision of the JP, the constable administered the county court in its judiciary and legislative functions. The constable was also in charge of enforcing orders from colonial and county officials in criminal as well as civil matters.[17] In many instances, the constable was not a paid position. Rather, the constable would be rewarded through a system of fees for recovering stolen property or providing various other services[18] such as supervision of elections, collection of taxes, and providing the public with notice of government actions and directives.[19]

# Chapter 4: Constables

In 1692, constables were under order to maintain well-working stocks in all towns of the colonies. The stocks provided public punishment of wrongdoers, whom the constable would, of course, be responsible for arresting.[20]

The law enforcement portion of a constable's duties was particularly important during this time. The county sheriff was often the only other law enforcement officer in the area. While sheriffs could make arrests and take other steps to enforce laws, they were often reluctant to do so. The main qualification they possessed to be the sheriff was that they owned a large estate. As wealthy gentlemen, they had little motivation to become involved in the criminal behaviors of those around them. Criminals were their peers or were too dangerous.[21]

On April 14, 1825, the first constable recorded as killed in the line of duty died in Venango County, Pennsylvania. Since 1900, there have been at least 130 constables killed in the line of duty across America. Texas leads the nation in this category with 25.[22]

## Constables in Texas

Constables made an early appearance in the law enforcement picture in Texas. The first constables were part of Stephen F. Austin's original codes for regulating criminal activity in the colony he had chartered with Mexico. Due to its colony status, Austin's codes received approval through the Mexican government and were then implemented.[23] Constables were thus one of the first officially recognized forms of law enforcement in Texas.[24]

The first man appointed constable under these new rules was Thomas V. Alley. He received his appointment in the year 1823 and had the distinction of being the first white man to serve in a law enforcement capacity in Austin's colony of Texas.[25] Alley's horse threw him and he drowned in the Colorado River in 1826 while fighting Indians.[26]

In March of 1836, the Constitution of the Republic of Texas created the office of constable in Texas.[27] The constable received specific mention in all nine constitutions that have existed in what is now the state of Texas, including three constitutions while the state was still a Mexican colony and one while Spain ruled Texas.[28] Many prominent citizens held the position of constable during this time, including John Austin and Juan N. Seguin.[29]

The current constitution for the state of Texas came into being in 1876.

Like all the other constitutions before it, the current one contains provisions for the office of constable.[30] Today, Article 2.12 of the Texas Code of Criminal Procedure defines the duties of constables as state certified peace officers.[31]

Despite their rise in importance in the area of enforcing laws during the early 1800s, in the aftermath of the Civil War it became increasingly difficult to fill these positions. Persons who received an appointment often refused to serve. The pay, equipment, and support for the constable were declining. All the way around, this position looked like more work, and dangerous work at that, than it was worth. This was especially true when the pay, equipment, and support for the county sheriff were rapidly increasing. The constable and the sheriff essentially traded responsibilities during this time, with the sheriff focusing more on law enforcement and the constable focusing more on administration.[32] The position of constable thus experienced a decline in prominence from which it has yet to recover.

The one notable highlight from this period appears to have been when El Paso Constable John Selman shot and killed John Wesley Hardin on August 19, 1895. Hardin, known as the Angel of Death, had killed over 30 people including several law enforcement officers. Selman had been hired by Hardin to kill a man who was married to a woman Hardin was sleeping with. Instead, Selman shot Hardin, ending his reign of terror across the Southwest.[33]

## Modern Constables

According to Lillian Alderete of the Texas Commission on Law Enforcement Officer Standards and Education, an estimated 780 persons currently hold positions as constables in Texas, .and another 3,563 as deputy constables.[34] The position of constable is a constitutionally created law enforcement office in the state of Texas with countywide jurisdiction in civil and criminal matters.[35] Elections occur at the precinct level in each county and authorize constables for regular law enforcement duties including investigations, patrol, and arrests.

The constable is the chief process server of the Justice of the Peace Court and serves a variety of judicial processes and notices, and is responsible for property seized under each action. Constables deal with civil process from various courts, including issues of forcible entry and detainers, writs of possession, citations, and executions issued from the Justice of the Peace Courts.

They can also process and execute misdemeanor traffic and hot check warrants of arrest for all types of municipalities and counties. Constables also assist any other law enforcement officer within their county.[36]

The position of constable derives from civil sources. In modern times, the role of the constable has reverted to an administrative position while the role of the sheriff has taken on the law enforcement duties. The role reversal has led many to see constables as having no value save that of serving civil process papers for the courts.[37]

## Qualifications to be a Constable

Constables receive certification as Texas state peace officers through the Texas Commission on Law Enforcement Officer Standards and Education (TCLEOSE). They must meet the same basic qualifications as all other peace officers in order to be certified. The voters of each precinct elect the constable every four years.[38]

Recently, the state legislature of Texas mandated that persons who are seeking the office of constable must possess an active or inactive state peace officer license or hold an Associate Degree from an accredited college prior to filing for election.[39] Persons not possessing an active license but elected constable must obtain an active license within 270 days or they may not serve as constable and must forfeit their office.

Additionally, in order to serve as a constable, the individual must possess a high school diploma or GED, and be eligible to for licensing under Sections 415.058 and 415.059 of the Government Code and Sections 1701.312 and 1701.309 of the Occupation Code.[40]

The County Commissioners Court can declare a constable position vacant if it has been vacant for at least seven consecutive years. Vacancy means having no person either running for office or receiving appointment to the office or having the person elected fail to meet the qualifications of the office during that seven-year time frame.[41]

Once the County Commissioners Court declares an office vacant, election or appointment cannot fill the office. Nor does the last person to hold the office continue to occupy the position. Records from a vacant constable's office transfer to the county clerk.[42]

The County Commissioners Court may reinstate an office of constable by a vote of the commissioners or by calling a special election of the precinct. An election must occur upon receipt of a petition signed by at least 10 percent of the qualified voters of the precinct.[43]

## Special Requirements

In addition to the normal peace officer requirements, the constable is required to complete some special continuing education classes specifically related to their main duties as civil process servers from the courts. During each two-year training cycle, all constables and deputy constables are required to complete a 20-hour course of instruction in civil process. Failure to complete this course demonstrates a form of incompetence and is thus grounds for termination. The civil process training requirement applies only to constables who took office after September 1, 1985. Constables who took office before this date and who have remained in office continuously are exempted.[44]

## Role of the Constable

The Texas Constitution, Article V, Section 18 states that each county with a population of 30,000 or more can divide into from four to eight precincts. Each precinct shall elect one Justice of the Peace and one constable, each of whom shall hold office for four years.[45]

In addition to the normal peace keeping duties of all Texas peace officers, the constables' duties include:

- Serve notice of termination of surety of public officials;
- Execute process issued by commissioners court;
- Execute subpoenas;
- Serve notices and citations in probate matters, and return;
- May serve notice on an attorney instead of party in probate proceedings;
- Notify landowner against whom execution is held, of need to set apart excess land from exempted homestead, accept designation, make due return, etc;
- Summon persons to a complete jury;
- Execute writ of sequestration and post copies of citation;
- Summon jurors for justice court;
- May appoint deputy constables;

- Cooperate with director of Texas Department of Public Safety;
- Execute all processes issued by the Texas Railroad Commission;
- Serve, process and execute orders of State Commission on Judicial Conduct[46]

The constable also has record-keeping duties related to the financial transactions of his/her office, fee collection, and other financial matters.

Constables are also responsible for normal policing duties such as peace-keeping, arresting offenders, patrolling, and criminal investigations.[47] Constables also normally cooperate with the other constables within their county in ways that are most beneficial to their constituents and county government.[48]

The constable's jurisdiction covers their entire county as well as every adjacent county and they may serve documents for state, county, and JP courts. The County Commissioners Court establishes fees for this service. Paid fees contribute to the general fund of that county.[49]

Constables have an additional power to recruit aid from the civilian population. If the constable's request for aid is not met, the civilian may face a civil penalty. The constable charges the person with contempt of court and the Justice of the Peace assesses a fine.[50] While the fine used to be only $10, the fine is now based on the judgment of the Justice of the Peace, and relates to the seriousness of the situation in which aid was refused.[51]

## General Grounds for Removal

Constables who fail to provide to the Commissioners Court evidence of possession of a permanent peace officer license on or before the 270th day after the constable takes office can lose their positions. They can also lose the position for failure to maintain a permanent peace officer license or stable surety bond while serving in office.[52]

Other grounds for removal include incompetence, official misconduct, and intoxication whether on or off duty. Immediate removal can occur in cases where the constable receives a conviction for a felony crime, or a misdemeanor charge of official misconduct.[53]

Removal from office also occurs through the voters of their precinct for a variety of reasons such as non-performance of the job, or failure to maintain a positive reputation. In some counties, the constable may also be subject to term limitations.[54]

## Current Duties

The duties of modern constables vary greatly according to their jurisdiction, especially the size of the population they serve. Constable departments in rural counties such as Crosby County may consist of only one officer with no deputies, no budget, and no resources. Departments in urban counties such at Dallas County may have large departments with many deputies and resources. The following sections compare the constable position in rural Crosby County with the same position in the urban Wichita County. Following this comparison, a brief discussion of several other counties gives a full view of the constable position as it exists in modern society.

Crosby County:

Crosby County is located in the panhandle of Texas, east of Lubbock. It is a mostly rural area with farming and ranching. The county has four precincts, but has only one constable, technically assigned to Precinct 2, but serving countywide.[55]

The most recent constable, J. W. Holbrooks, has held this position for 34 years. This is not his first policing job, but obviously his longest. What is more remarkable is that for 34 years now he has been paid only one dollar per year for his services. Officially, he receives a fee of three dollars for each time he serves court papers to a member of the public. During his long tenure as constable he has only done this four to five times however, as the county sheriff's office normally handles this duty. This means his entire salary for 34 years adds up to less than $50![56] For many, the question is why would he do this job? The simple answer is that he loves his job.

In fact, Mr. Holbrooks holds a regular, non-law enforcement job as his main form of employment. He works full-time for the water district at White River Lake. In this capacity he reads water meters, repairs broken or leaking pipes, maintains public restrooms in the camping areas, and deals with other public water issues. The water district provides him with a regular salary and a small house so he is located on site.[57]

While on the surface these two jobs seem to have nothing in common,

# Chapter 4: Constables

the reality is that they are a really nice blend. White River Lake is a small lake with camping, boating, and fishing activities, all of which require regulating. Additionally, a hunting prohibition exists on water district property, thus requiring monitoring for poaching and other hunting violations including trespass and possession of unlawful weapons. These activities all take place on water district property and require a permit issued by the water district. The water district, however, does not have the power to commission a peace officer to do these jobs. Therefore, the water district encourages Mr. Holbrooks to hold the constable position and act as Lake Ranger.[58]

Constable Holbrooks is the only law enforcement officer stationed in the White River Lake area. Sheriff's deputies, game wardens, and other officers patrol the area infrequently, and Constable Holbrooks is normally on-call 24 hours a day. He goes to work for the water district every morning and the day unfolds from there.[59]

White River Lake has few permanent residents, but upwards of 50 vacation homes that are not occupied full-time. Since the homes around the lake are largely empty during the regular week, owners rely on Constable Holbrooks to maintain a level of surveillance. He can normally accomplish this in the scope of his water district job. Many of his calls for service also involve checking homes for security and responding to burglaries. He frequently calls property owners to report unsecured buildings and other odd circumstances such as property damage.[60]

The bulk of Constable Holbrooks' law enforcement duties thus revolve around crime prevention and community service. He does, however, engage in a variety of investigations, mostly concerning burglaries and thefts. He also makes arrests and writes tickets. Over the past seven to eight years, he has averaged two to three arrests per year and 10 tickets per year. Most commonly, these cases have involved three categories of offenses: drunkenness, poaching or other hunting violations, and trespassing. Occasionally domestic violence cases will also occur.[61]

Constable Holbrooks also responds to accidents involving motor vehicles including boats and jet skis. There have been 14 deaths due to these types of accidents during the time Holbrooks has been constable. Many were alcohol related.[62]

Constable Holbrooks engages in a wide variety of daily activities, blending a civilian job with a law enforcement job in a way that allows him to focus on community service and crime prevention activities. He spends a large amount of his time in positive interactions with the public as they enjoy the recreation available at White River Lake. The rural area and accompanying lower level of crime afford him the ability make his position more supportive and less punitive than many other law enforcement positions in the state.[63]

Constable Holbrooks officially retired from his position at the Water District and his position as constable in November of 2010. His position at the water district filled quickly, but his position as constable remains empty as of this writing.

## Wichita County:

Wichita County is located in North Texas, just below Oklahoma. The county population is over 131,600 persons, reflecting an increase of 7.6 percent since 1990. Within the county are several urban cities including Wichita Falls, Burkburnett, Iowa Park, and Electra. Each of these cities has a population of over 3,000. Wichita Falls is the largest city in the county with a population of roughly 106,000.[64]

Constable Mark Brewer works in Precinct 1 of Wichita County. Whereas the constable in Crosby County is paid one dollar per year, in Wichita County the constables are paid $42,000 yearly plus given a vehicle and insurance. The deputies' salaries range from $34,000 to $38,000 per year. The county also pays their personal health insurance.[65]

Constable Brewer has held his current position since 1985. His office also employs three paid deputies and two reserve deputies. Precinct 1 covers two Justice of the Peace courts, truancy issues for the school district, and enforcement of child support orders from the State Attorney General. Additionally, court papers from both the district court and out of area courts process through this office. Each person in the department handles a specific section of these duties thus ensuring full coverage.[66]

The following passages by Constable Brewer demonstrate some of the variety of duties that will occur in a constable's day:

"September 7, 2007 started out like any other day, up at 5:30, a 10-mile bike ride in the county, quick shower and shave, then off to work. A quick stop at the office to see what is waiting, then off to the coffee shop for a cup. Knock on a few doors, serve a few papers & before you know it, it's lunchtime. 1:00 p.m., time to check by the office, catch up on phone calls, do paperwork.

## Chapter 4: Constables

Explain to an attorney what the difference is between exempt & non-exempt property and why I will not seize a defendants' homestead under a writ of execution unless the attorney directs me to do so in a letter on his stationery. A funny thing I've learned, attorneys will ask you to do a lot of things one is not allowed to do & when you ask for a letter by them directing you to do it, the letters (along with the request) fail to materialize.

"It's now four-thirty & time to go serve mental commitments at North Texas State Hospital. After forty-five minutes, time to go home, cook supper & help kids with homework.

"Eight p.m., the phone rings. It's the dispatcher. SRU (special response unit) call out. My Chief Deputy and I are team members. An ex-deputy sheriff says he has a hostage and wants to kill a Burkburnett Police Officer but a deputy will do. I think to myself 'This is going to end badly' and say a quick prayer asking God to protect the team & resolve this peacefully. I did not want this to be 'suicide by cop.' I call my Chief to insure he got the call out message & headed out to the scene.

"Garland and I arrive about the same time. We learn there is no hostage and are assigned the responsibility of inner perimeter security along with reconnaissance. Our team sniper is set up so we leave our M-4 carbines in our vehicles (a very bad tactical mistake that will bite us in the ass later). We take up a position 50–75 yards from the front of the trailer house in a bar ditch. About ten minutes later, the suspect steps outside, points a .45 auto in our direction and fires the weapon. Garland & I get as low as we can in the ditch checking to make sure both of us are unharmed. I remember thinking, 'You are trying to bait us into killing you Scott, & I don't really want to kill you, I'm not taking the bait.' A few minutes later he pulls out an SKS rifle, points it in our direction & fires. I heard a bullet whiz by my head & kick myself for not bringing my carbine with me. I am outgunned & in a bad position and have quickly changed my mind on not wanting to hurt him. I want to do whatever I can to keep from getting myself and Garland shot by an SKS. I think 'it's dark so he really does not know exactly where we are. If I fire at him with my Glock, he will know exactly where I am.' It was dark & I did not have a decent sight picture, so in spite of my desire to return fire I hunker down even lower. Garland & I check with each other to make sure we are both OK. We give each other the 'thumbs up' sign. Over the next fifteen minutes, several more shots are fired in several directions by the suspect. Suddenly I hear the sound of a .308 rifle going off & the standoff is now over. I know the suspect is dead, having committed suicide by cop. I grabbed my medical bag because as team medic I am responsible to treat not only team members but also suspects who are injured. I check the suspect; he has no pulse & I see that he has suffered injuries incompatible with life & declare the area a crime scene.

"Four a.m., the scene has been cleared, time to go home & prepare for what the day will bring. Typical day? Like I said there is no such thing."[67]

As indicated in the quotation above, the constable of Wichita County has a larger department, a larger budget, and a greater emphasis on punitive types of law enforcement and court service than the constable does in Crosby County.

### Other Counties:

As in Crosby and Wichita Counties, constables across Texas work a wide variety of duties. The salary and resources available to them also vary widely.

Ben Adamcik is the constable in Precinct 3 of Dallas County. He has been in law enforcement for the past 41 years in the Dallas area. He says the number one priority for his department is to hold the department with respect.[68]

Adamcik says, "There are three courthouses in his precinct, which house 49 deputies. There is a civil division, traffic division and warrant division. Both Civil and Warrant divisions give out more than 8,000 citations every month." The warrant division is responsible for the mental illness division. The civil division handles about 99 percent of the other warrants while the mentally ill make up 1 percent. The precinct also serves out an estimated 14,000 evictions per year.[69]

Routine traffic stops represent a large portion of the Dallas County Constable's workload. Fines from these traffic stops reached an excess of $25.8 million in 2008. This represented a 250 percent increase from 2003. The vast majority of this increase directly relates to the work of the constables. The money from these fines helps the city make up for any budget shortfalls they experience in the turbulent economy.[70]

Traffic enforcement by the constables is not without critics. Questions arise concerning the expansion of the constable's powers, the use of "speed traps," and the infringement of the constable into an area of enforcement already handled by city police. Supporters see increased enforcement making the roadways safer and the increase in fines as relieving a potential tax bur-

# Chapter 4: Constables

den.⁷¹ Despite the controversy, Dallas County Constables continue to write large numbers of tickets for traffic violations.

Laredo County presents a different focus for the constable's office. Constable Augustine Juarez of Webb County (Laredo) has seven deputy constables underneath him. The most rewarding part of his job is serving citations, not writing them. He likes helping the people of Laredo. Truancy seems to be a main problem in Laredo. It is an everyday occurrence.⁷²

A beginning constable in Webb County is paid $8.25 per hour. This places them in the middle of the salary range between Crosby County and Wichita County.⁷³

Alvie Hester, constable of Precinct 4, Tom Green County, says the hardest part of being a constable is the disrespect for the office that the public had in the past. "Back then if you said you were a Constable, you would hear snickering. That really hurt. Since then, we have worked hard to bring a more positive image to being a Constable."⁷⁴

Hester has been in law enforcement since 1983. The sheriffs' departments in Concho County, Sterling County, and Tom Green County have employed him. "Being a Constable requires you have 20–30 more hours above what is requested by TCLEOSE. I find myself spending 90 percent of my time dealing with civil matters. I have four Deputy Constables that deal mainly with mental health issues. When they receive a call they do a welfare check, interview the individual and then make a decision if the individual needs to be taken to a hospital."⁷⁵

"I love being a Constable. Last year I wrote about 1,000 citations. I don't have to take people to jail. I can give them a citation and leave," says Hester.⁷⁶

As can be seen, constables across the state engage in various duties including serving civil papers and handling truancy. They do these jobs under widely differing circumstances relating to wages, staffing, and resources. Additionally, the amount of each type of duty they will perform differs by the community they serve. The constable position is thus like many other law enforcement duties: similar, yet different depending on where the constable serves.

## Mental Health Duties

Among the many duties assigned to constables across Texas, according to Koca,[77] in at least one county in Texas (Tom Green) the constable also serves as the mental health peace officer. Mental Health Constables handle all cases regarding persons with mental illnesses, including all complaints about such persons, serving of commitment papers, transporting to mental facilities, and welfare checks on such persons. Local area law enforcement agencies refer all cases concerning mentally ill persons to the mental health constables who are on call 24 hours a day.

Mentally ill persons pose special challenges for law enforcement. Many are not able to control their behavior and so create disturbances. Others are unable to understand what law enforcement officers want from them. Some will attempt suicide or become dangerous to others around them. Mental facilities with severe budgetary constraints are coming under increasing pressure to release patients who can supposedly behave in a stable manner with medication. The lack of aftercare in the community creates a pressing need for law enforcement officers with the special skills and training needed to effectively deal with the patients who have returned to the community but have destabilized, and those persons in the community who develop a need for mental health services.

Tom Green County has four electoral precincts. In 2001, the constables were asked to take on the mental health peace officer duties when the local police and sheriff's office indicated they did not with to take on the duties. Two of the four elected constables took on the mental health peace officer duties for the entire county. Largely these duties have fallen on their deputy constables.[78]

The county judge supervises the mental health peace officer program in Tom Green County. This is a natural outgrowth of the close working relationship between the constable and the judge. It also stems from the fact that the county judge must sign off on all cases where a mentally ill person is committed to an institution.[79]

There are currently four deputy constables assigned to work with the mental health cases. Each receives specialized training including a TCLEOSE course, 4001 Mental Health Worker, followed by a period of on-the-job training with an experienced officer much like a Field Training Officer program in regular policing. The period for formal training and field training varies by officers, largely due to skill and motivation.[80]

Mental health constables work rotating shifts five days a week and are on call roughly two days a month. While on duty, they are responsible for all calls to any law enforcement agency concerning persons with mental health issues. This may include suicidal persons, persons in need of civil commitment, and persons in other ways needing the attention of law enforcement officers due to their behavior.[81]

One of the practical problems with having all mental health peace officer duties in the offices of two constables is that budget and manpower constraints are often critical. One of the most common tasks is transporting mentally ill persons to an appropriate facility. According to a deputy constable of Tom Green County, "By law we are required to take the mentally ill to the nearest mental health facility, but because of such variables as funding, prior stays, and available bed space this is often not what occurs. The trip we make most frequently is to Big Spring and it is 88 miles one way from San Angelo. We send one deputy (because of manpower) and that is whether you are transporting one or four. We take juveniles to Wichita Falls more frequently than any other location (Big Spring does not treat children or juveniles). Wichita Falls is approximately 490 miles from us and when they are on diversion, we take our juveniles to El Paso, which is 894 miles. We also use the facilities in Kerrville, Austin, San Antonio, Rusk and Lubbock when Big Spring is on diversion."[82] When the constable or deputy constable on duty is undertaking such a trip, the entire county is often without the services of a law enforcement officer who specializes in dealing with the mentally ill. The deputy constable continues:

The main goal of this unit is to provide crisis intervention and stabilization for the mentally ill through jail diversion. We frequently receive calls to intervene when a mentally ill person has come into contact with law enforcement and it is obvious that taking this person to jail will not do any good because they are often not aware of what they have done or that it is wrong. We do, of course, have our element of criminals which have attempted and learned to work the system to avoid doing more time or for other reasons.

The only other thing I wanted to point out about our unit is that we are required by law to drive unmarked units and wear plain clothes. This is in part due to confidentiality issues involving the subjects we deal with and secondly because it is a proven fact that even the mentally ill generally know who the police are and associate them with someone being in trouble or having done something wrong. I have shown up on many calls with the police department on the scene and the subject is barricaded and having a wild fit because the police are there to harm them. They will not calm down or even attempt to listen to these officers. As soon as I get to them and begin to talk to them, everything changes. The fact that I am not wearing a uniform with all the bells and whistles seems to calm them. They do not even seem to notice the gun and badge. I am simply someone to talk to and someone that can help them."[83]

## Conclusion

Despite the decrease in status constables suffered in the 1800s, the position has persisted and even thrived. The elected constable in modern day Texas is a peace officer who performs a wide range of duties including regular law enforcement, civil process serving, and dealing with violators with mental health issues.

The position of constable recently received recognition as extremely important in the scope of Texas law enforcement. On March 1, 2005, the Texas State Senate adopted a resolution proclaiming the date to be Justices of the Peace and Constables Day.[84]

Today, we see the state legislature requiring more and specific continuing education for constables in order to help them perform the myriad functions expected of them. There is also a new variety of optional training courses designed specifically for constables, including the Constables Leadership Development Training offered through the Bill Blackwood Law Enforcement Management Institute of Texas (LEMIT).[85]

Between the official recognition by the State Senate and the enhanced requirements, the position of constable seems to be regaining its lost status. The future indeed looks bright as constables expand their duties to include mental health peace officer tasks. It seems certain that as society's needs grow and change, the constable position will continue to play a vital role in Texas law enforcement.

SSA Larry Diaz during a train safety training.

*Photo Courtesy of Johnnie Holbrooks.*

# Chapter 5

# Railroad Police

## Introduction

The laying of the first train tracks in America began on July 4, 1828. By May of 1869, trains could run all the way from the east coast to the west coast.[1] Today trains carry millions of people every year. Amtrak alone carried 28.7 million persons between October 2007 and September 2008. Amtrak is thus the largest passenger rail system in America and ranks eighth overall in passenger transportation when compared to domestic airline travel.[2] During 2008, Amtrak carried 323,210 persons through 19 stations across the state of Texas.[3]

Trains also carry billions of tons of cargo each year. The Burlington Northern Santa Fe (BNSF) Railway operates an average of 1,200 freight-hauling trains each day. These trains are composed of roughly 190,000 cars.[4] This is only one company covering 28 states and 2 Canadian provinces, but it gives some idea of the size of the train industry.

## History of the Position

Railroads have played an important part in making America the country it is today. When first built, trains could carry more cargo and persons, farther and faster, than any previous method of land transportation. The railroad also played a significant role in westward expansion.[5]

Old-time rail transportation frequently appears in a romantic light, especially in western-style movies. There were serious problems however. The first train robbery in the United States occurred on October 6, 1866, when the Reno brothers robbed an eastbound train in Indiana, emptying one safe and throwing another off the train. Train robberies such as this one became more popular, with some robbers derailing the train to get it stopped.[6]

Even before train robberies became an issue there were crime problems facing the new industry. Property damage, employee theft, accidents, and other issues accompanied the progress trains were bringing to civilization.[7] Railroad police were the answer to many of these problems. Allan Pinkerton became involved in these crime issues in the early 1850s. His contract with Rock Island, Galena & Chicago Union, and Illinois Central railroad companies specified his duty to create his own agency to handle problems for them. The Pinkerton Detective Agency got its humble beginnings from this contract. The reputation of the agency developed rapidly, especially after agents foiled the 1861 assassination plot against President-elect Lincoln.[8]

With the rise in proprietary police for railroad companies, Pinkerton moved his agency into other realms. The Pinkerton Detective Agency still exists today, although its connection to railroad companies is now limited at best.

Throughout the rest of the 1800s, railroad policing was accomplished through a confusing assortment of men ranging from those hired for their proficiency with a gun to those employed through a professional company like the Pinkerton Detective Agency.[9] A few exceptions existed however.

The first official railroad police officer received a commission in 1865 in Pennsylvania when the state passed the Railroad Police Act. The governor held the power to commission officers recommended to him by the railroad companies. Officers commissioned in this manner held the same police powers as municipal police officers in Philadelphia. The Act further specified the badge officers would wear and the manner in which the commission could be revoked.[10]

Thirteen years later, famed gunfighter/lawman Bat Masterson hired 100 officers to provide protection for Santa Fe Railway crews who were feuding with crews from the Denver and Rio Grande Railway. In railroad circles, Masterson holds fame as the first chief of the Santa Fe Railway Police.[11]

Railroad policing hit a high point in the 1940s. Between the United States and Canada, there were roughly 9,000 officers from 400 railroads. They covered 225,000 miles of mainline tracks and untold miles of lesser side tracks.[12]

The decline of the railroad police began in the 1950s with the completion of the interstate highway system. Many persons who had formerly relied on train transportation were now choosing to drive. Additionally, American railroads underwent federal deregulation in 1980. Many railroad companies merged or ceased to exist. This created a dramatic decrease in the number of railroad companies.[13] Corporate downsizing and increasing technology have also contributed to the reduction in the number of railroad police.[14]

## Railroad Police in Texas

According to the Bureau of Justice Statistics, in 2004 there were 18 mass transit/railroad policing agencies nationwide. These agencies employed 3,094 full-time, sworn officers.[15] Of these officers, 101 hold commissions in the state of Texas.[16] Many of the other officers will also work part-time in Texas, but will hold a law enforcement commission from another state.

There are over 12,000 miles of railroad tracks in the state of Texas. Along these miles of track, the nation's highest number of collisions, injuries, and fatalities occur. In 1999, for example, an Amtrak passenger train outside Eagle Lake, Texas, collided with a tanker truck. Both locomotives and seven of the 10 cars derailed. Eighteen people were injured and 800 feet of track were damaged.[17]

Collisions and derailments, while dramatic, do not form the bulk of the work for railroad police. Their work normally centers around less deadly events. This does not mean they do not face danger in their job. At least four railroad police officers in Texas have lost their lives in the line of duty. Thomas Henry Bennett died from gunshot wounds on September 11, 1910. Twelve years later, on September 6, 1922, M. V. Torres also died from gunfire. Both men worked for the Texas and Pacific Railroad Police Department.[18] John Phillip Barber of the Dallas Terminal and Railway Company Police Department died from gunshot wounds on September 21, 1945.[19]

William W. Garrett of the Forth Worth and Denver Railroad Police Department was the only one of the four not killed by gunfire. Garrett died September 12, 1927, because of vehicular assault.[20] It is interesting to note that all four men died in the month of September.

## Modern Railroad Police

Individual railroad companies in America have operations spanning several states. The BNSF Railway for instance covers 34,000 miles of train tracks in 28 states. The vast majority of this territory is 100 feet wide.[21] Other companies have a similar situation, often on the same set of tracks.

Literally hundreds of other law enforcement agencies may also have jurisdiction in the area of the railroad. Cooperation with these agencies is imperative if the railroad police are to be successful in their duties.[22]

Modern railroad police are unique in the world of law enforcement. They hold positions with a private company, yet hold licenses as state peace officers. Additionally, they receive a federal retirement.[23] They are non-union and can retire at 60 years of age if they have 30 years of service.[24]

## Qualifications to be a Railroad Police Officer

Law enforcement authority for railroad police lies in both state and local rules. Interstate authority exists through Title 49 USC 207.5.[25] Persons applying for positions as railroad police will need to meet the criteria set forth under these laws in order to be eligible for employment.

As railroad police work for private companies, hiring procedures and initial qualifications for the job may vary. However, some basic criteria may be used. Generally, applicants must be 21 years of age, possess a valid driver's license, and pass a background check, physical exam, psychological exam, and drug screening. For most companies, applicants must also have passed a basic peace officer academy. Prior law enforcement experience is desired but may not always be required.[26]

Many departments will also require potential officers to possess a number of college credits or a college degree. Additional academy-type training or on the job training once hired is also a common requirement.[27]

Railroad police officers' primary law enforcement training and commission resides in the state where they live or work.[28] Officers who are commissioned in Texas will meet the criteria discussed in Chapter 2 and will be granted a special commission through the Texas Department of Public Safety and the Texas Railroad Association.[29] Officers working for the same company but commissioned from another state will be subject to different types of initial training depending on the rules of their commissioning state.

## Special Provisions

The property owned or used by a given railway company frequently covers more than one state, and multiple jurisdictions within each state. The ability to work in all areas where the railway company has property is an absolute necessity in order for the officer to be effective. Under Title 49 USC 207.5,[30] railroad police may extend their jurisdictions beyond their commissioning state to cover all areas where their company owns property.

This does not mean there are no limits to their jurisdiction or their power within that extended jurisdiction. The following represents a summary of the powers of the railroad police under Title 49 USC 207.5:

- The railroad company has provided official notice to the non-commissioning state of the officer's credentials;
- Officers engage in enforcement only of laws relevant for protection of railroad employees, passengers, patrons or property;
- Officers engage in regulation of interstate, intrastate, or foreign transportation on the railroad or its property;
- Officers engage in regulation on railroad property of the movement of personnel, equipment, or goods needed for national defense;
- Officers engage in pursuit of a criminal who moves off railroad property;
- Officers engage in other police purposes as defined in state or local laws.[31]

Another special provision available to railroad police officers comes from Public Law 106-110,[32] which allows railroad police officers to attend FBI law enforcement training. This is not a requirement, but an opportunity. Amtrak sends all of its officers for this training.[33] Other agencies may select a few of their officers for this special training.

As can be seen, railroad police have much broader jurisdiction than most other law enforcement officers do. They in fact resemble federal officers in this capacity more so than they resemble local officers, even though they hold licenses locally through state agencies.

## Role of the Railroad Police

Railroad police resemble other police agencies in that they allow officers to specialize in various areas. For the BNSF, these areas include K-9 handler, firearms instructor, driving instructor, defensive tactics instructor, and field training officer. Since 9-11, specialization may also occur in the area of Homeland Security.[34] For Union Pacific, specializations also cover the areas of Accident Analyst, Haz-Mat, Crossing Accident Reduction Enforcement (CARE), Grade Crossing Collision Investigation (GCCI), and SORT team (SWAT).[35]

Railroad police are often involved in prevention efforts. These efforts frequently involve data analysis and development of strategies for crime reduction, protection of personnel and property, and accident avoidance.[36] Railroad police are thus more proactive than many other policing agencies that rely on calls for service to dictate their workload.

This does not mean railroad police do not respond to calls. As with all policing agencies, railroad police cannot ignore calls for service, and it is often the calls for service that create the data used to develop prevention programs. Calls can also serve as an opportunity to meet the public and provide services to them.[37]

In addition to dealing with crime, railroad police are involved in emergency response coordination where railroad property or trains are involved. Derailments or natural disasters such as tornadoes, hurricanes or ice storms can severely disrupt train service.[38] Events such as these will often involve working with other agencies. Therefore, developing and maintaining good working relationships with other law enforcement agencies is essential.

## Current Duties

While train robbery is not generally a pressing concern in modern society, there is a wide variety of other concerns with which railroad police deal. The duties of today's railroad police officer range from data analysis to public education to arresting criminals and testifying in court.[39]

Many railroad police agencies employ K-9 teams. The use of dogs in this type of law enforcement is similar to their use in other policing contexts. Searches for contraband and persons around trains and railroad property are a major function for railroad K-9 units. Crime prevention through presence and officer protection are also common railroad K-9 functions.[40]

Railroad officers must be self-motivated and responsible persons. They work alone most of the time, and are frequently in remote areas with little or not backup. They must frequently work long hours, but since they are on salary, they do not receive pay for this overtime.[41]

As with all law enforcement officers, railroad police have a great deal of discretion over their actions. The isolation of this job makes proper use of this discretion an imperative. In many cases, the railroad police officer will even have the discretion to set their own working hours.[42] This situation would be easy to abuse, which makes maturity and self-motivation a necessity to succeed in this job.

**BNSF Railway:**

As mentioned earlier, the BNSF Railway Company covers 28 states and 2 Canadian provinces. Within the 28 states, there are between 160[43] and 175[44] railroad police officers working for the company. A beginning senior patrolman's salary is roughly $47,000.[45] Salary moves upwards from there through the six-figure range.[46]

While the terrorist attacks of 9-11 did not target the railroad industry, the effects have carried over to areas outside of air transportation. BNSF Railway has a designated team of officers who are dedicated to terrorism prevention activities.[47] Additionally, K-9 teams are now trained for both patrol and explosives detection.[48] Knowledge of terrorist methods and trends is now necessary for railroad police.[49]

The Resource Protection Team provides security for the BNSF Railway. They are responsible for all security measures for the company and its assets. The Police Solutions Team is the law enforcement division and includes police personnel and K-9 units.[50]

Charles Matthews is a Chief Special Agent with the BNSF Railway. When he began his career as a railroad police officer, he was with the Atchison, Topeka and Santa Fe (ATSF) Railway Company. ATSF and BN Railways merged in 1995 to become BNSF and Matthews continued his career with this company, having now served as a railroad police officer for 15 years.[51]

In his daily work, Matthews supervises police services in a nine-state area. Additionally, he is responsible for the K-9 program and leadership of the Southwest Corridor Police team of 54 persons. In this capacity, one of his responsibilities is to maintain communication with railroad executives, most of whom are not policing personnel.[52]

The most vivid memories of Matthews's time with the railroad police center on large-scale disasters such as hurricanes, derailments, or significant criminal events. As an administrator, part of his duty is to undertake problem analysis and program development to prevent these sorts of incidents.[53]

Special Agent in Charge Luis Mares also works for BNSF. Mares began his career in railroad policing 17 years ago with the Santa Fe Railway Police where he served as K-9 handler Senior Special Agent. After the merger created the BNSF Railway, Mares continued as a K-9 handler. Currently he serves as Special Agent in Charge of the BNSF Railway K-9 team, stationed in El Paso, Texas.[54]

When asked how his workday is spent, Mares[55] replied "As the Agent in Charge I am mostly in an administrative role. I oversee K-9 training and certification, and daily station operations. I coordinate travel of the Agents due to task force operations, which are frequently held to apprehend burglary rings operating throughout the country, etc."

Most memorable to Mares[56] are "the K-9 searches for trespassers hiding on trains. My best K-9 train search yielded over 70 undocumented aliens apprehended. That is with one man, one dog and a lot of luck. It took more than 9 Suburbans to transport them."

Union Pacific:

Like the BNSF Railway, Union Pacific Railway operates over a large territory, covering 23 states. They employ roughly 215 railroad police agents, 60 of whom hold primary assignments in Texas. A beginning agent with a college degree and three years of prior law enforcement experience will start with a salary of $65,000.[57]

Senior Special Agent David Green began his career with railroad policing in 1978 with the Missouri Pacific Railroad. Like many railroad companies, this company merged with Union Pacific Railroad in the middle of the 1980s. Green continued his career, becoming a K-9 handler and accident analyst.[58]

Currently, Green is a territory agent covering the area of Texas from Weatherford to Pecos. "I am on call 24/7 and can set my work hours as needed. I answer all calls on my territory, thefts, train riders, rock throwing, shooting at trains, etc., but I specialize in crossing accident investigations. Most locomotives have cameras now and they all have a black box similar to planes."[59]

Cameras and black boxes will help an investigator determine exactly what happened before and during a train wreck. These pieces of technology require computer skills to use them effectively. This is one of the many areas in railroad policing that demonstrate a need for officers to keep learning and expanding their skills.

## Public Education

Current duties for railroad police also include public education through such programs as Citizens for Rail Security.[60] This program began in 2006 and currently has 6,525 members. It involves citizens who are interested in the railroad industry and in trains. These volunteers go through a short training program, which teaches them to recognize security violations, unusual circumstances, and trespassers on railroad property.[61]

Employees of BNSF have a similar training program called On Guard. Between the two programs, reports of potential suicides, stolen equipment, and items left on the tracks including vehicles, have increased. Reports of trespassers and lost children found near the tracks have also increased. The potential crimes and disasters prevented through these programs cannot be overestimated.[62]

In addition to public education, railroad police engage in educational programs with other law enforcement agencies. These efforts include the Grade Crossing Collision Investigation program and Operation Lifesaver.[63]

Operation Lifesaver is the national rail safety organization. Its purpose is to train rail safety coordinators to operate programs to reduce collisions, death, and injuries relating to trains and tracks. The rail safety coordinators take their training and return to their home states to set up their own statewide programs.[64]

Statistics from a recent survey of Texans by Operation Lifesaver demonstrate the importance of this program. Crossing railroad tracks while warning lights were flashing and driving around a lowered crossing gate appeared to be acceptable to 30–45 percent of those surveyed. An additional 20 percent indicated more acceptance of going through a gated railroad crossing than of running a red light.⁶⁵ Obviously, there is need for more education about the dangers of these activities.

The public education function of railroad police officers helps to make the railroads and trains safer and more accessible to the public. Engaging members of the public, other law enforcement agencies and non-enforcement employees of the railway company in safety issues enhances the measures the railroad police can engage in. These persons serve as an extra set of eyes and ears for the railroad police. The general public in particular seems to hold a fascination for trains and these programs allow them to learn more about the subject and more actively pursue their interests.

## Homeland Security

Railroads are a large portion of the nation's critical infrastructure. Recent attacks on subway and passenger rail around the world have highlighted the need to focus on security for rail transportation in the United States. Until recently, the focus has been all about aviation security, with rail security left to state or local officials, generally in the form of railroad police.⁶⁶

The Department of Homeland Security has recently expanded its efforts in the area of transportation to include passenger and freight rails. Homeland Security's efforts fall into the four core areas of funding, training and deploying of manpower, development and testing of new security technologies, and security assessments.⁶⁷

Local personnel are being included in training and funding. Amtrak alone received $7.2 million in fiscal year 2006 to provide extra security in three of their major service areas.⁶⁸

Freight hauling along rail lines is also receiving intense scrutiny. New technologies aim at detecting chemicals and explosives and enhancement of cargo container inspection through the use of K-9 teams and screening technologies.⁶⁹

A large amount of funding, training, and physical equipment is available to local law enforcement agencies including railroad police. The railroad police are already on the front lines of securing our nation's rails. Homeland Security's needs can only serve to enhance their position.

## Conclusion

Railroad police officers are unique in the world of policing. They are required to be part businessperson, part police officer, and part public educator. Railroad police officers are frequently an unknown to the public, often working alone and in remote areas. As Matthews[70] indicates, however, once with the railroad police, few ever leave for another policing position.

In the post-9-11 world, security for public transportation has taken on increasing importance. Cargo security has also increased dramatically. Homeland Security initiatives focusing on rail security cannot help but filter down to railroad police who continue to evolve to meet these challenges now and in the future.

Racing Commission Director of Enforcement Mike Gougler.

*Photo courtesy of Mike Gougler.*

# Chapter 6

# Racing Commission

## Introduction

The racing of horses and dogs has a long and distinguished history, with horseracing often referred to as the sport of kings. In fact, both sports have centuries of history. Horseracing may be one of the oldest sports known to man, with its beginnings before the written word.[1]

Many of the same issues that arise with other professional sports have occurred within the world of racing. Gambling, doping, and other illegal practices require regulation in order for any sport to maintain integrity with fans. In the state of Texas, these issues have become the work of the Texas Racing Commission.

## History of the Position

While there are many similarities in the issues surrounding the racing of dogs and horses, their evolutions were quite separate. A brief history of both sports may therefore be instructive.

Greyhound Racing:

Greyhounds are an ancient breed of dog. Evidence shows a strong connection to ancient royalty, particularly in Egypt. King Tutankhamen, Queen Hatshepsut, and even Cleopatra all owned Greyhounds.[2]

In addition to the royal connection, Greyhounds have the distinction of being the only breed of dog mentioned by name in the Bible.[3] Proverbs 30:29–31 discusses a Greyhound as one of four things that are attractive when in motion. The other three are a lion, a goat, and a king.[4] The idea of racing Greyhounds may thus relate to Biblical times.

Greyhound racing's original name was coursing. The Romans and the Celts both practiced the sport around the time of the Roman Conquest of Britain. The coursing races of this period involved a single dog chasing a game animal. By the sixteenth century, coursing involved two dogs chasing the same animal to see which dog was fastest.[5]

Coursing became an official sport in 1776 at Swaffham, England. The rules allowed only two dogs and one hare per race. The hare received a 240-yard head start to ensure the race was a real contest.[6]

The oldest coursing race in continuous operation is the Waterloo Cup Meet. This race has occurred every year since 1837. In its heyday, the race attracted crowds of 75,000.[7]

Greyhounds had come to America at least as early as 1848. George Armstrong Custer kept a pack, which he was coursing the evening before the Battle of Little Big Horn in 1876. Dogs belonging to one of his former officers set a record in 1878 when four dogs ran down six out of twelve antelopes in a herd.[8]

Coursing Greyhounds spread across the country as settlers moved west. In local fairs and celebrations, informal Greyhound races were as common as horse races.[9]

Some thought coursing with a live animal as prey was cruel. In 1876, the British had experimented with a fake hare, but the race was not popular so the British abandoned the effort.[10] Thirty-one years later, in 1905, Owen Patrick Smith of Hot Springs, South Dakota, attempted to use an artificial hare and an oval track in order to make the sport both less cruel and more popular. Smith continued to work on his concept for several years, perfecting the artificial hare and moving around the country to spread the idea.[11] Greyhound races under Smith's model in Tulsa, Oklahoma, produced the first champion dog in the country. In the early 1920s, Mission Bay won 28 of 30 races in his career.[12]

Smith finally achieved permanent success with Greyhound racing when he took it to Florida in 1922. The first track he built became the famed Hialeah Racetrack. Although this track would ultimately be more famous for Thoroughbred racing, it was the spark that set off a worldwide fascination with Greyhound racing.[13]

In 1925, Charles A. Munn received exclusive rights from Smith to use his fake hare for Greyhound racing in England. Munn went on to form the

Greyhound Racing Association in 1926. Under his guidance, there were 68 dog tracks in England by 1928.[14]

In Florida, pari-mutuel betting on Greyhound races became legal in 1932. Massachusetts followed suit in 1934. Fifteen states now have Greyhound tracks, while seven states have banned the sport. Iowa, Rhode Island, and West Virginia tracks make most of their money on slot machines rather than the races themselves. As racing revenues have declined, other states are pushing for expanded gambling opportunities such as slot machines.[15] The issue of gambling in this area remains unsettled.

Horseracing:

Nomads in Central Asia first domesticated horses around 4500 B.C. Horseracing followed quickly, appearing in the earliest forms of human records. Mounted horseraces and horse-drawn chariot races both appeared officially at the Greek Olympics in 638 B.C.[16]

European horseracing development really emerged after the Crusades of the twelfth century. Men returned from the Crusades with Arabian horses which they bred to the English horses of the day and the breed of Thoroughbred emerged. This breed is known worldwide for its combination of speed and endurance.[17]

Professional horseracing came to England during Queen Anne's rule from 1702–1714. Control over British racing has rested with the Jockey Club since 1750. This group continues to set all rules for racing and racecourses even today. The Jockey Club is also involved in regulating the breeding of racehorses, keeping the General Stud book since 1793. Only horses descended from those listed in the book may hold the title Thoroughbred and subsequently be allowed to race.[18]

The first racetrack laid in America was on Long Island in 1665. Development followed along the British lines, with an American Stud Book emerging in 1868. By 1890, there were 314 tracks across the country. An American Jockey Club came into existence in 1894 to battle the corruption that was flourishing in the largely unregulated American system.[19]

Thoroughbred horse racing in America is commonly associated with the state of Kentucky. The first official track opened in Lexington, in 1789. Almost 100 years later, the track at Churchill Downs opened. This track is perhaps most famous for the Kentucky Derby.[20]

The first winner of the Kentucky Derby was a three-year-old named Aristides. The chestnut colt's trainer was Ansel Williamson and his rider was Oliver Lewis. Both men were African American.[21]

Horseracing currently comes in a variety of forms including harness racing, steeplechasing, and Quarter Horse racing. Thoroughbred racing remains the most popular, with race distances ranging from three-quarters of a mile to two miles.[22]

In America, horseracing is the second most popular spectator sport, with baseball being the most popular. In 1989, the various tracks in America put on a combined 8,004 days of racing, with an estimated 56,194,565 persons in attendance. Betting on horse races topped $9.14 billion in that year.[23]

Racing Enforcement:

The American Jockey Club is the premier rule-setting authority for horseracing in the United States. This group also has ultimate authority to set regulations concerning breeding of Thoroughbred horses.[24] Horseracing is not, however, the only type of racing. Therefore, other agencies help to cover the full spectrum of racing needs.

Gaming/racing law enforcement represents a small area of specialization, with six agencies and 225 full-time sworn officers nationwide as of 2004.[25] The Texas Racing Commission is one such agency, currently employing seven full-time sworn officers.[26]

In the realm of horseracing, state agencies, such as the Texas Racing Commission, share the authority to appoint racing officials and to supervise racing rules with the American Jockey Club. Setting of racing dates and licensing of participants in horse- and dog racing remains solely with the state agency.[27] Control over gambling regulation also resides with the state agency.

Gambling:

Gambling is a large part of the draw that racing holds for the public. For both dog and horseracing, the pari-mutuel system of wagering exists at all tracks in the United States. Pierre Oller created this system in the late nineteenth century.[28]

For each wager, a fixed amount, generally 14–25 percent, pays for track expenses, taxes, and other fees. The amount left is divided by the number of wagers to determine the amount of payoff for each bet. These are the odds.

The first number in an odds statement is the amount of money available for winners of this bet. The second number is the bet amount required to receive that payout. Odds listing of 2-1 means a payout of two dollars occurs for every one dollar that was bet.[29] In this situation the bettor would double their money.

The type of bet placed also affects odds. In horseracing for example, a person may bet on a horse to win, place, or show. There are also bets involving more than one race. The daily double involves choosing the winner of two consecutive races. Exactas are bets choosing the first and second place winners in the same race. Pick six bets involve choosing the winning horses in six consecutive races.[30] The more difficult the bet the more money the successful bettor will make. Winning a pick six will pay more than winning a single race bet.

Ensuring proper race procedures and fair betting practices is an important aspect of maintaining integrity for racing sports and the tracks where racing occurs. The Texas Racing Commission has taken on this responsibility for the Greyhound and horseracing industries in the state.

## The Texas Racing Commission

Senate Bill 15 created the Texas Racing Commission in 1987, although appointments to the Texas Racing Commission did not begin until the following year.[31] The commission originally had six regular members and two ex-officio members. The six regular members received appointments from the governor and consisted of two veterinarians, two Greyhound-racing specialists, and two horseracing specialists. The ex-officio members were the chair of the Public Safety Commission and the Comptroller of Public Accounts.[32]

Article 3 of the Texas Racing Act of 1986 established the powers and duties of the Texas Racing Commission.[33] All of these duties apply to horse or Greyhound racing, and the wagering that may occur at said races. The various sections of Article 3 cover issues relating to licensing, drug testing, supervision of races, rule creation and enforcement, and record keeping.[34]

The Texas Racing Commission is composed of an Executive Director, General Counsel, and Enforcement, Racing and Veterinary Departments. These five areas work together to ensure the safety and legality of racing and betting in the state of Texas.[35]

The Executive Director is the face of the agency, appearing before the legislature and other government bodies. Along with the General Counsel, the Executive Director coordinates the evaluation of racetrack license applications, recommends race date allocations and assesses penalties for violations by racetrack licensees.[36]

The General Counsel provides legal advice to the commission and represents the agency at State Office of Administrative Hearings as prosecutor for appeals rising from decisions of stewards and judges. The General Counsel also coordinates commission meetings and rulemaking proceedings.[37]

The Chief Veterinarian who supervises the other veterinarians and the test barn supervisors at racetracks heads the Veterinary Department. The Chief Veterinarian works with the Animal Health Commission, the American Association of Equine Practitioners, and the Texas Veterinary Medical Association on issues of common concern. Pre-race inspections of all animals, inspections of kennels and stables, and implementing the commission's drug-testing program are also coordinated through this department.[38]

The Racing Department consists of the stewards and racing judges involved in the live races at Texas racetracks. These individuals oversee races and determine finish orders. They are also responsible for overseeing persons licensed for various occupations at racetracks. Stewards and judges may discipline licensed persons with up to $5,000 fines and/or up to one-year suspensions.[39]

On October 6, 1989, the first racetrack under Texas Racing Commission jurisdiction opened at G. Rollie White Downs in Brady, Texas.[40] By January of 2003 Texas had three Greyhound tracks and seven horse tracks.[41]

## Qualifications to be a Racing Commission Investigator

Investigators for the Racing Commission must be licensed peace officers who have met the requirements set out in Chapter 2. Knowledge of animals and the racing sport will certainly be helpful. Experience with a variety of investigative subjects is also desirable, particularly in the areas of vice enforcement.[42]

The pressure to have a background in investigations is immense. The first several officers hired as investigators were all former police officers who had extensive experience in vice enforcement, organized crime task forces, or other related areas.[43]

## Special Requirements

As originally formulated, the Texas Racing Act did not provide for Enforcement Department personnel to hold commissions as peace officers. Only track stewards could carry this commission. The first stewards were thus peace officers. The qualifications for peace officer and the racing knowledge needed to be a steward rarely comes in the same person, however. Consequently, an amendment to the Texas Racing Act passed in 1991, allowing investigators within the Enforcement Department to be peace officers. Stewards subsequently ceased carrying peace officer commissions.[44]

## Role of the Racing Commission

Many of the divisions of the Racing Commission are administrative in nature. Making rules for racing, setting dates, and interpreting regulations form a core of their activities. The Enforcement Division is essentially the action arm of the commission. The following is a summary list of the duties the enforcement division of the Texas Racing Commission will perform:

- Investigate positive drug tests on animals
- Conduct criminal history checks on license applicants
- Investigate illegal wagering
- Investigate use and possession of contraband
- Investigate drug abuse and narcotics trafficking
- Investigate other illicit activities[45]

## Development of the Enforcement Division

On February 16, 1989, John T. Williams assumed the position of Director of Enforcement. Williams had been with the Dallas Police Department for over 25 years when he retired to assume the position. During his time with the police department, he served in several special units devoted to vice crimes and organized crime.[46] This experience had already exposed him to enforcement tactics for many of the crimes he would find in the world of racing.

Bill Meincke was Executive Secretary for the commission and served as director when he hired Williams to head the Enforcement Department. Meincke had been director of the New Mexico Racing Commission in his previous position. He played a major role in uncovering a serious horse-doping problem in New Mexico during the mid 1980s. Meincke sent Williams to New Mexico for two weeks of training at the start of his job. Texas was committed to having a clean racing program with a strong drug-testing component. New Mexico had dealt with the underlying issues in creating such a program under Meincke so this was a good training ground for Williams.[47]

In the beginning, Williams had to be involved in everything including computer programming of a Case and Intelligence Tracking System. The Enforcement Department had to create its own forms and establish guidelines and procedures.[48] Williams essentially built this department from the ground up.

## Current Duties

Mike Gougler is currently director of the Enforcement Department. The Texas Department of Public Safety (DPS) previously employed Gougler, where he worked extensively with the polygraph (lie detector) division. He accepted his current position after retiring from DPS.[49]

According to Gougler, the work of the enforcement officers on non-race days is composed mostly of paperwork concerning background checks, criminal histories, and other issues related to licensing tracks, track owners, and all other persons who are involved in the sport. Much of this work occurs through cooperation with the Texas Department of Public Safety.[50]

On race days, the enforcement officers get an early start to their day, patrolling the barns and other back areas of the track. Officers look for contraband and persons known to have a criminal record. They will also check licenses and accompany the veterinarians on rounds to check for animal doping, animal health, and animal readiness for racing. The officers have a lot of authority to search without a warrant. All vehicles, barns, tack rooms, etc. may be searched. Only searches of the living quarters of the personnel require a warrant.[51]

During the race, the enforcement officer may be in the steward's tower, watching the starters and jockeys to ensure the race is not fixed. Enforcement officers will also watch the betting to further ensure fairness.[52]

During Quarter Horse races the officers will watch for shocking devices that may be used by dishonest jockeys to spur their horse unnaturally. Rough riding by jockeys receives careful monitoring to ensure that jockeys do not interfere with other horses and jockeys in the race. Enforcement officers are also responsible for checking equipment to ensure obedience to rules and regulations.[53]

According to Gougler,[54] most persons involved in the sport, be it horseracing or dog racing, want an honest race. The enforcement officers are ultimately concerned with maintaining the integrity of the sport and the health and safety of the participants. Enforcement officers will often develop close working ties with members of the racing community and may even develop a network of informants. This allows the officer to be more effective in knowing what to search for, where to search, and when illegal behaviors are likely to happen.

Texas is the most restrictive state where racing is concerned.[55] Around 90 percent of the cases Texas Racing Commission officers become involved in are violations of commission rules resulting in fine or suspension.[56] Enforcement officers will prepare the case the same way any other detective would. Mostly this involves following up on paperwork and histories of violations.

Persons holding any job at a racetrack from the track owner to the janitor to anyone involved with the animals must hold a license through the commission. Licensing includes fingerprinting and a background check completed by the Enforcement Department. A serious criminal record could keep a person from being licensed.[57]

All animals and all licensed persons may be subject to drug testing. The Veterinary Division is in charge of the testing of animals. A commission-approved laboratory conducts testing of personnel. The Enforcement Division is not involved in the actual testing itself, but may become involved in ordering tests or in investigating any tests that come back positive for an illegal or banned substance.[58]

At the end of each race, officials conduct drug testing on the first and second place animals. A random sample of the third-place animals also become subject to testing. If the tests result in a positive finding, the enforcement officers will conduct an investigation.[59]

Enforcement Division officers cover particular tracks for the racing season. As the season progresses, agents can move from track to track as needed.[60] Larger races may require more personnel. Any race or racetrack in the middle of a doping scandal or other criminal behavior can expect to have more attention.

Enforcement officers are required to work with any other law enforcement agency that may have jurisdiction where the track in question is located. Specifically, Section 3.11 of the Texas Racing Act requires officers to share intelligence data with other states and agencies. Cooperation under this section also requires help to be forthcoming by commission members when any other law enforcement officer is engaged in enforcement of any section of the act.[61] This forces officers to maintain good working relationships with other law enforcement agencies.

A good working relationship with other agencies makes sense when the crimes most commonly associated with racing are considered. Any drug activity in racing will have connections to the outside world. Betting scandals frequently have a connection to larger crimes such as extortion or organized crime. The world of racing does not exist in a vacuum and the Racing Commission officers will do well to remember that.

According to Gougler,[62] racetracks are like small communities. All the crimes found in other small communities occur at racetracks. In addition to the normal criminal matters, issues of animal cruelty and other race-specific crimes will occur. Normal criminal matters routinely receive referral to DPS or to the local policing agency. This frees the Racing Commission enforcement officers to focus on regulatory issues.

Effective enforcement has, in some cases, led to criminal behaviors moving off-site. For example, Gougler[63] has seen animal handlers pull off the side of the road to dope the animals before entering racetrack property. Enforcement officers thus need to be aware of what happens off-track as well as on-site. Cooperation with local law enforcement becomes a key to solving this type of crime.

## Conclusion

The Texas Racing Commission is a small agency within the scope of law enforcement. The Commission has only ever had seven investigators and job openings are not common.[64] Even with this small size, the investigators play an important role in keeping racing and the associated betting free of crime and scandal.

Through cooperative efforts with other agencies, the impact of the investigators has the potential to be enormous. Homeland Security has yet to enter into the area of racing enforcement. However, as can be seen in other areas of law enforcement, keeping terrorists from making money through racing may become a priority in the future.

Inspector Larry Gray.

*Photo Courtesy of Larry Gray.*

## Chapter 7

# Cattle Brand Inspectors

## Introduction

Societies as far back as the ancient Egyptians practiced the branding of animals.[1] The brand is essentially a label denoting ownership, rather like a serial number on a laptop.

An array of laws and rules developed around the branding of animals to ensure proper branding, use of different brands by different people, transfer of ownership for a branded animal, etc. Regulating and enforcing these laws now falls to the Cattle Brand Inspectors, licensed peace officers with expertise in livestock.

## History of the Position

A brand registry became the most convenient way of ensuring each person, ranch, or company used a separate brand. In the United States, the earliest brand registry still in existence is from Richmond County, St. George, Staten Island, New York. The registry includes brands, court cases, road surveys, and other municipal information. Although the earliest brands in this registry are not dated, they appear to come from 1678.[2]

Each state and several federal agencies including the Department of the Army, now have procedures for brand registry and inspection. Each state and federal agency follows its own rules.[3]

## Cattle Brand Inspectors in Texas

Texas has a rich history of involvement in the cattle industry. Cattle theft was virtually an industry. Thieves normally received a fine of $20 as punishment. In order to pay this fine, the thief would steal more cattle.[4]

The wide-open ranges of Texas in the era before barbed wire fencing made cattle theft an easy occupation. This was particularly true for yearling cattle that did not yet have brands. The problem was of such a magnitude that branding and official brand registry seemed a likely answer. Unfortunately, thieves simply moved on to altering brands and theft continued.[5]

The first recorded brand in the state occurred in Gonzales County and dates to 1832. Like many things in the state of Texas, branding took on its own flavor. Road brands came about in Texas as a way to mark ownership during the large-scale cattle drives that moved herds to market. Once these drives gave way to more efficient transport, this brand ceased to exist.[6]

Texas also used a county brand on the neck of an animal. This seemed like a great deterrent to cattle thieves. Not only would the stolen animal need re-branding, but also the new brand would need registering in the county where the cow had originated.[7]

As animals changed ownership legally, their brands would need to change. A vent brand applied to the animal indicated this change in ownership. The new brand indicated who now owned the animal.[8] Fortunately for most cattle, ownership did not normally transfer repeatedly.

Cattle theft became a felony in Texas in 1873. Additionally, driving improperly branded cattle to markets became a crime carrying a fine of up to $2,000. Killing an unbranded cow without a proper bill of sale also became a crime. Altering brands and illegal marketing or branding became equated with cattle theft and carried the same penalty.[9]

The most common brand in Texas is the letter O. An O exists by itself or with other letters/symbols in 850 different brands.[10]

### The Texas and Southwestern Cattle Raisers Association:

In 1877, 40 leading cattlemen in North Texas banded together to form the Stock Raisers Association of Northwest Texas. This group encouraged oversight of shipping and marketing of cattle in order to deter theft.[11] Issues dealt

## Chapter 7: Cattle Brand Inspectors

with by this early organization also included whether or not to allow Mexican cattle imports.[12]

As more cattlemen joined the association, it became apparent that the scope of authority was too limited to be effective. At a meeting in Fort Worth in 1883, a committee of five inspectors was established, thus creating the Cattle Brand Inspector we know today.[13]

Brand inspectors needed to be impartial judges of ownership for cattle. However, persons possessing stolen cattle tended to be violent as well as criminal. Therefore, brand inspectors also needed to be armed lawmen.[14]

Cattle Brand Inspectors made an impact almost immediately. In four years, the association paid $54,000 for their services. In that same period, the inspectors had recovered 1,016 stolen or stray cattle, amounting to roughly $74,000 in savings.[15]

In the late 1890s the association successfully lobbied to have their Cattle Brand Inspectors commissioned as Texas Rangers. This status was supposed to bring greater respect and more enforcement ability to the position. It did not, however, prevent the inspectors from meeting violence at the hands of cattle thieves.[16]

The association was involved in efforts to protect the interests of the smaller rancher as well as the larger one. This included protection against unfair shipping prices sought by railroad companies. The association convinced the Interstate Commerce Commission (ICC) that railroads had been unfair to all members of the cattle community. In 1905, the ICC granted the association the right to seek repayment of the overcharges for association members.[17]

By the late 1880s, Texas had 16 associations representing the interests of the cattle industry. Communication and transportation issues were steadily improving, however, and many of the smaller associations disbanded as members joined other associations. The Stock Raisers Association of Northwest Texas held a meeting in 1893 where the subject of representation for the association emerged. The idea of expanding to cover more areas of Texas as these other associations disbanded brought on discussion of the association's name. The result was a name change to "The Cattle Raisers Association of Texas." The scope of the association also changed to include all of Texas, Indian Territory, Oklahoma, and New Mexico.[18]

The Panhandle and Southwestern Stockman's Association remained independent of the state association until the early 1920s. It was the last such independent organization in the Texas cattle industry. Several years of drought had hit the industry hard. Economics and other hardships drove the associations together, with the state association assuming leadership. The merger inspired another name change to recognize the new role of the state association as truly representing all the members of both organizations. Between the two, members came from Texas, New Mexico, Colorado, Arizona, and Oklahoma. The new name became "The Texas and Southwestern Cattle Raisers Association." This name has remained unchanged since the 1921 meeting.[19]

In 1943, the Secretary of Agriculture designated the association as the official brand inspection agency for the cattle industry of Texas. Association operations expanded quickly after this, making the association the premier organization of its kind. The most complete system of brand inspection in the cattle industry now resides with this association.[20]

In court cases involving cattle theft, an attorney hired by the association may assist the prosecutor. There is no charge to the member involved in the case for this service.[21]

Texas law requires brands to be re-registered every 10 years. It remains illegal to use brands that are not registered.[22] Failure to properly register a brand can also mean exclusion of the brand as evidence of ownership in court.[23]

The Inspectors:

In the early years of the association, inspectors manned stations strategically along routes commonly used for driving cattle to markets or to better grass areas. Recovery of most stolen cattle occurred along these routes. Local ranchers would often serve as backup, standing armed guard around a herd as the inspector checked brands and sales records.[24] This situation indicates the high level of support shown for the inspectors.

During large-scale drives, groups of inspectors would gather, particularly near the Red River. The group could inspect several herds rapidly. On one occasion, the inspectors found 176 head of stolen cattle in one herd.[25]

Rail shipping of cattle created shipping points where inspection could be easily undertaken. At their peak, the stockyards in Fort Worth handled up to 7,500 head in a single day. Cows with multiple brands were common, averaging three brands per cow. The record appears to be a cow in San Antonio with 37 distinct brands on its hide.[26] Inspectors in Fort Worth would have been very busy with 7,500 cows and 3 brands each making an average of 22,500 brands to identify and inspect each day.

Cattle brand inspection was not always a safe occupation. The first Cattle Brand Inspector killed in the line of duty was Tom Peeler. Cattle rustlers shot him to death in 1897. Peeler had found a group of rustlers with a herd of stolen cattle outside Campbellton. One of the murderers received a 25-year sentence for this crime.[27]

Other inspectors were murdered either in the line of duty or in other circumstances. The cold-blooded murder of two more inspectors occurred on Easter Sunday in 1923, while the two sat in a hotel lobby in Seminole. Both men had widespread reputations for being excellent detectives and determined law officers. The public uproar that followed their murders was immense.[28]

In the aftermath of this tragedy, inspectors received a corps of assistants who, while not always law enforcement officers, were helpful in recording brands and expanding the availability of information on the cattle industry to prevent cattle theft. This was especially important as the cattle industry expanded and membership in the Texas and Southwestern Cattle Raisers Association (TSCRA) grew.[29]

Cattle rustling has changed over the years and the job of the Inspector has evolved to meet this challenge. Cutting strays during a drive to market has given way to behaviors resembling poaching. Now a rustler might kill a cow, cut its hindquarters away and leave the rest hidden in the scrub for predators to eat. The rustler could be long gone, even for days, before evidence of the crime emerges. The inspector can hardly perform the job by waiting at a trail head for a herd to be driven by.[30]

## Modern Cattle Brand Inspectors

The Texas and Southwestern Cattle Raisers Association currently has 29 Special Rangers in the Texas and Oklahoma districts. These rangers work in specific districts within their states and work closely with local, state, and federal law enforcement agencies in cases where livestock is involved.[31]

The districts covered by the Special Rangers contain anywhere from 7 to 27 counties as determined by human and cattle population. Such large areas require a good working relationship with these other law enforcement agencies.[32]

The Texas and Southwestern Cattle Raisers Association generates funds entirely through membership dues, with roughly 15,000 members in Texas and Oklahoma. They do not receive state or federal funds. Cases handled by the Special Rangers do not have to involve persons who are members.[33]

## Qualifications to be a Cattle Brand Inspector

Special Rangers in the state of Texas hold commissions through the Texas Department of Public Safety. The Oklahoma State Bureau of Investigation commissions Special Rangers in Oklahoma. Each group has statewide jurisdiction in their commissioning states.[34]

Additional requirements include a minimum of five years prior law enforcement experience including investigative experience. Each applicant undergoes a background check as well. One of the most important qualifications is having experience in the cattle industry. This last requirement seems to be the hardest qualification for potential applicants to meet.[35]

## Role of the Cattle Brand Inspectors

Primarily, Special Rangers are responsible for livestock theft. The theft of items related to livestock is an included duty. As a secondary function, the Special Rangers supervise market inspectors.[36]

Special Rangers are also involved in education programs relating to prevention of livestock theft. Training in procedures for proper branding is also available to interested parties.[37]

## Current Duties

Larry Gray has been a Special Ranger with the Texas and Southwestern Cattle Raisers Association for 28 years. Gray began his law enforcement career at 19 years of age when he became a police cadet during college. His first law enforcement job was with the Fort Worth Police Department where he eventually attained a position in the Criminal Investigations Division of the fugitive/special crimes unit.[38]

Gray began his career as a Special Ranger in 1981. Gray grew up on a ranch and around the cattle industry; thus, the position seemed a nice blend of his family background and his law enforcement career. He originally served in the Fort Worth District, covering Dallas, Tarrant, and adjacent counties. He then transferred to the Graham District. In 1995, he received a promotion to Director of Law Enforcement in Fort Worth.[39]

Special Rangers have a great deal of variety in their jobs, but it comes with a price. According to Gray, "While the job seems glamorous from the outside it many times requires long hours and nights away from home. The Special Rangers put in a lot of windshield time and average driving approximately 3,500 miles per month covering their districts. A typical day for a T.S.C.R.A. Special Ranger can vary from conducting criminal investigations to visiting the auction markets within their districts and visiting with producers."[40]

Special Rangers inspect somewhere between five and six million cattle each year. Special Rangers rely on 70 to 80 market inspectors at 130 livestock markets to assist them with this work. Results of inspections reside in a computer database that represents the largest database of its kind. Over 700 law enforcement agencies nationwide request information from this database each year.[41]

Over 15,000 brands exist in Texas, and the Special Ranger must be able to positively distinguish each one.[42] As of 1997, inspectors are also responsible for monitoring the two horse-processing plants in the state of Texas. Each year these plants receive 35,000 horses. Inspection of each horse ensures it is not stolen.[43]

Special Rangers also work closely with county sheriffs to handle local cases involving cattle. This cooperative effort is necessary considering the size of the territory that a Special Ranger may have to cover. Additionally, the Special Ranger may assist other state or federal law enforcement officers in cases where livestock is involved.[44]

Cattle Brand Inspectors are many times a cross between rancher and peace officer. The continued requirements for branding of cattle combine with the continued presence of cattle thieves to ensure that these inspectors will continue to be important in the world of law enforcement.

Their success is obvious. In 2009, Inspectors in Texas and Oklahoma worked 1,022 cases. They recovered stolen livestock and ranch equipment valued at over $4.8 million, including 3918 head of cattle, 57 horses, 14 trailers, 24 saddles, and 43 other pieces of equipment.[45] The cattle industry desperately needs these inspectors.

## Conclusion

Members of the cattle industry in Texas have held Cattle Brand Inspectors in high esteem since the beginning. They have proven their worth by regaining stolen cattle and equipment, and by deterring theft.

As a token of the esteem held for Cattle Brand Inspectors, Colt created a Brand Inspector Centennial Commemorative Colt .45 in 1983 to honor the 100th anniversary of the creation of Cattle Brand Inspectors. The gun was a limited edition of only 150. Each gun has 50 prominent brands, a miniature badge, the names of past association presidents who were still alive, and the name and brand of the purchaser engraved upon it. These guns were among the last .45s that Colt ever manufactured.[46]

As well respected as the position of Cattle Brand Inspector is, it becomes more difficult each year to find persons with the combination of police skills and knowledge of the cattle industry. The position will remain necessary, however, as long as cattle remain a moneymaking industry.

Sul Ross State University UDPS Officer Grace Strachan.

*Photo taken by Lorie Rubenser.*

# Chapter 8

# University Police

## Introduction

Of all the law enforcement positions covered in this book, readers are probably most familiar with campus police. Most likely readers are now or were at some point college students and, therefore, had at least limited exposure to campus police.

College campuses are supposed to be places where people go to learn new things and explore their futures. Parents sending a child to college for the first time tend to be reasonably concerned about their child's safety. The college student may also have concerns for their safety. This is where campus police can play a major role.

## History of the Position

University police departments cover a wide variety of institutions including two-year colleges, four-year colleges, universities, and medical schools. In 2004, there were 764 such agencies across the country, employing 14,416 full-time, sworn officers.[1]

The earliest known form of campus security dates back to the fifteenth century at Oxford University in England. Campus administrators appointed officers labeled "Bedels" to serve writs, collect fines, and make arrests. Maintaining order on campus included keeping lists of offenders and the heavy use of punishments and fines. Fines may have been particularly popular as the Bedels' salary came directly from them.[2]

In America, official forms of campus security arose in 1894 at Yale University in response to a growing authority problem between students and administrators. The existing informal methods of control, including a student group referred to as the Blue Skin Club, were proving inadequate.[3]

In the post-Revolutionary War period, the mission of higher education had become more nebulous. Student cultures had changed as well, moving away from preparation for the ministry and into other intellectual fields.[4] A sort of generation gap ensued, bringing conflict to higher education.

The figurative straw that broke the camel's back was a riot in 1894 that occurred between the students and the local townspeople. Rumors had surfaced that the medical students were digging up recently buried bodies from the local cemeteries to use in their coursework. By the time the riot was over, many persons on both sides had been injured.[5]

In this time of unrest, Yale University began paying local police to patrol the campus at night. Many of these officers were subsequently hired to form the Yale Campus Police.[6] City officers had heretofore been reluctant to conduct patrols on campus. The students knew this and would often hide from police by returning to campus after committing some offense in the town.[7]

The first official campus police officers in America were Jim Donnelly and Bill Wiser. Both men were veterans of the New Haven Police Department, and both had volunteered for assignment at Yale. They began the job in September 1894, just before the fall semester began. The biggest challenge was overcoming the resistance of the students.[8]

When Donnelly and Wiser succeeded in winning over the students, other officers from the New Haven Police Department pushed for assignment at Yale in their places. Donnelly and Wiser resigned from the New Haven Police Department in the face of this pressure. They received appointment as special constables for Yale and designed their own uniform. The Yale University Police Department was thus an official entity.[9]

Prohibition brought extra chores for the campus guards. These included dealing with alcohol violations, enforcing curfew, and regulating dormitory visitation policies—especially visits by members of the opposite sex.[10] Despite these complicated duties, for most universities, campus security up through the 1950s appears to have been a function of night watchmen. These men commonly worked for the physical plant or grounds department and would undertake minor repairs, check locks, and watch for fires while on duty.[11]

Development of campus security, or policing, really took off after WWII.

The student demonstrations of the 1960s were a major spur in this trend. Philosophical changes also contributed as students asserted their rights, sex segregated dorms were no longer the norm,[12] and entire campuses became racially integrated. The law enforcement aspects of campus security helped to overcome the deficiencies of the watchman system, much in the way municipal policing of the past had moved forward.

## University Police in Texas

No records exist for proof, but the University of Texas (UT) might have been the first university police department in the state of Texas.[13] The campus police at UT began in 1968. Currently there are 130 employees in the department,[14] making it one of the largest in the state.

As of 2006, 93 colleges and universities in Texas had their own police departments.[15] Sworn personnel within these departments accounted for 2,166 positions.[16] In other words, 31.58 percent of the full-time sworn personnel in the state of Texas work for colleges or universities.

## Modern University Police

Modern university police departments are responsible for providing a variety of services to the campus community. Crime control and order maintenance are important, but may not be the bulk of the work required of the officers. Service delivery, safety issues, and other duties relating to the mission of the university are often more prevalent.

Many colleges and universities own property or have operations on property not physically connected to their main campus site. Campus police hold jurisdiction in any county where their school owns property. This allows them to provide full coverage, even though most of their work occurs on the main campus.[17]

Campus police often work with other law enforcement agencies. This can occur during routine daily work where officers provide backup for one another or it can be a special program or specific crime problem. For example, campus police may work with officers from the Texas Alcoholic Beverage Commission (TABC) on alcohol-related programs. TABC also routinely disposes of alcohol seized by campus police.[18]

## Qualifications to be a University Police Officer

Persons interested in applying for positions as university police officers must meet the criteria for a state license as a peace officer. See Chapter 2 for a detailed discussion of these criteria. Additional requirements include passing a background check and possessing a valid driver's license. Many departments will require a certain level of education, up to and including a bachelor's degree.[19]

## Special Requirements

Requirements will vary by agency, but most agencies will have additional requirements if an applicant is seeking a position above entry level. Positions as sergeants, lieutenants and chiefs will normally have additional requirements. These requirements can include advanced levels of peace officer certification, higher levels of education, and years of experience.[20]

## Role of the University Police

Ultimately, the role of the university police is to keep campuses safe. This occurs through presence at large events, crime investigation, building lockups, parking enforcement, and other services. Many smaller schools will have their campus police department operate the vehicle registration system, the school ID system, key control, and fire safety.[21]

College students commit an estimated 80 percent of campus crimes. Fortunately, these crimes usually do not involve a weapon. Today, college orientation programs across the nation are focusing on student violence, including components on how to stay safe and be alert to crime.[22]

One thing that students are now aware of is that most perpetrators are students themselves. The majority of perpetrators and victims also readily admit that they would have never been in that situation if it had not been for the use of alcohol or drugs.[23] Campus police are now increasingly involved in efforts to educate students about the dangers of alcohol and drugs.

## Current Duties

Angelo State University:

Angelo State University (ASU) emerged in 1928 as a two-year community college. It achieved university status in 1965. The school became part of the Texas Tech University System on September 1, 2007.[24]

ASU is a medium-sized school with 6,387 students, located in San Angelo, Texas. The university offers over 100 programs resulting in an associate of nursing degree, 40 bachelors' degrees, 23 masters' degrees and one doctoral degree.[25]

The main campus sits on a 268-acre site. The university also has a 6,000-acre farm at an off-site location. The farm has a meat production laboratory and other classroom facilities.[26]

Police Chief James Adams has over 20 years in law enforcement and previously served as captain with the Baylor University Police Department in Waco, Texas. He has been with the Angelo State University Police Department for seven years. He takes pride in what he has achieved in the short time he has been with Angelo State.[27]

The men and women of his department have a longstanding tradition of providing quality services to the campus community. Adams is proud to lead this talented and dedicated group of professionals. The police department is committed to serving the campus community, creating an environment where all can be safe and succeed.[28]

Currently the university's police department employs 26 persons in addition to the chief. One officer is dedicated only to parking enforcement. Thirteen other officers engage in general policing duties. The department also employs eight public service officers and four communications operators.[29]

Adams is especially proud of the great progress the department has made. During his tenure, the police department has grown and become a progressive, modern campus police department. Accomplishments include the expansion of the department's fleet, purchase of a new radio system, implementation of laptops in patrol units, and numerous other resource upgrades. In 2008, the department moved to its own building, which doubled the amount of space available for offices. The new site also contains an expanded communications center. Adams credits the accomplishments to teamwork throughout the ranks and a dedicated staff.[30]

ASU has a Director of Environmental Health, Safety and Risk Management (EHSRM). In addition, that department just hired an Emergency Management Coordinator to oversee the university's emergency plans and preparedness. The office of EHSRM reports directly to the Vice President for Finance and Administration. The police department is also in that division and answers to the same VP.[31]

The university's Onecard office reports through Adams. The Onecard office is responsible for issuing campus IDs and managing building access through the use of a card reader system.[32]

Angelo State University is shifting to become a residential campus rather than a commuter campus. This means building more dormitories and requiring more services related to residential living. The campus police department recently received authorization to hire more officers to keep up with the new demands created by the new residential facilities. Filling these new officer slots is a challenge, however, as many area departments are trying to hire new officers. Competition among employers is tough.[33]

Sul Ross State University:

Sul Ross State University (SRSU) opened in 1917 as a state normal college located in Alpine. Classes began in 1920 with 77 students.[34]

The school received its name from Lawrence Sullivan Ross, a former soldier and Texas Ranger. Ross also pursued a political career, first as sheriff, then as state senator and then as governor. Ross moved on to be president of what is now Texas A&M University. Ross died on January 3, 1898.[35]

The normal school at Alpine became Sul Ross State University officially in 1969. During the 1970s, programs were added in Uvalde on the campus of Southwest Texas Junior College. These programs now exist as the Sul Ross State University Rio Grande College (RGC).[36]

In the fall of 2008, SRSU had 1,834 students enrolled in 48 undergraduate and 27 graduate programs.[37] The main facility sits on a 93-acre site in Alpine. The university also has 554 more acres in Alpine, a 468-acre working ranch, and the branch sites for RGC in Uvalde, Eagle Pass, and Del Rio.[38]

The University Department of Public Safety (UDPS) office is in Alpine. SWTJC police or local municipal police handle policing issues on the RGC properties. UDPS in Alpine maintains crime statistics for RGC, even though they do not actually handle the crimes themselves.[39]

Sul Ross State University began a program of campus security in 1927 when the campus engineer, Charles Young, took on security duties. The program then developed much in the same way as campus security at Yale University. In 1945 the first paid night watchman, Walter P. Hayes, was hired.[40]

It was not until 1951 when a campus security department emerged at SRSU. Campus police came along in 1960. The passing of Senate Bill 162 in 1967 created the requirement that the university have a real security department. The Chief of Security position emerged at this time, but sometime between 1976 and 1982 the title changed to Chief of University Police.[41]

At least two persons who were Chief of University Police at SRSU originally hired on as academic instructors. Larry Graham and Timothy Postin both gave up their academic appointments for their policing positions. Both lasted approximately two years or less before leaving SRSU entirely.[42]

Currently the department employs a director, a lieutenant, five officers, two civilian employees and eight to ten student workers. Salaries range from $22,700 for the civilian employees to roughly $52,000 for the director. A beginning officer can expect to make around $24,010. Civilian employees may earn extra pay through longevity increases. Sworn personnel may earn longevity and hazardous duty increases.[43]

The current Director of Public Safety at SRSU is Johnnie Holbrooks. He has been with UDPS since 1987, becoming director in August of 1996 after working his way up the ladder. His tenure with UDPS has been one of the longest if not the longest of anyone in the history of the department.[44]

Since beginning his career with SRSU, Holbrooks has seen the department move from Campus Police to University Department of Public Safety. Public Safety is supposedly a more user friendly and less intimidating title.[45]

As described by Holbrooks, the UDPS officer at SRSU can engage in a wide variety of tasks. A partial list includes:

Unlock vehicles, raise flags, facility unlocks/lockups, monitoring sporting events, maintaining patrol vehicles, purchase of equipment, scheduling, maintaining relationships with University departments and local law enforcement agencies, issuance of parking citations, booting vehicles, parking control, traffic control, investigation of incidents/offenses, arrests, safety inspections, Physical Plant work orders, Uniform Crime Reports, State Office of

Risk Management surveys/inspections, Texas Department of Insurance/State Fire Marshal inspections, opening elevators, responding to fire alarms, conducting fire drills, re-setting fire alarm panels, submitting/process offense/incident and call slip reports, coordinating street lamp/lamp post checks, daily crime logs, crime/safety alerts, call slip status reports, deterrence, refer incidents/offenses to Student Life, collect information of crimes/incidents from local law enforcement agencies.[46]

There is always something for the officers to do.

Student workers in the SRSU Department of Public Safety may write tickets for parking violations on campus. Currently a ticket for not having or improper display of a parking permit costs $10, up from $2. Handicap parking violations are $50, up from $25. The tickets do not affect the normal driving record/insurance, but can result in administrative penalties like withholding of grades if not paid. According to Holbrooks, people complained more often about the $2 tickets of the past than about the $10 tickets currently used.[47]

Unusual things happen to campus police officers despite the routine appearance of the job. Holbrooks recalls:

I had a report of big javelina on campus. My Lieutenant and I located it behind the Morelock Academic Building. It had no intention of moving. The Texas Parks & Wildlife was called to assist in dealing with it. My Lt. went into the building in attempt to open a window and scare it away. I was maintaining a pretty good safety distance by the Warnock Science Building when I observed a male subject walking in the general direction of the javelina. My Lt. scared the javelina causing it to jump over a rock wall heading directly towards the male subject and myself. I told the male subject to run. The male subject and I both ran. The javelina veered off and ran off in a different direction and was later captured without incident by the Texas Parks & Wildlife. Another time an officer and I were called to the Turner Range Animal Science parking lot during the intercollegiate rodeo in regards to finding skinned hands and feet. College rodeo contestants were sure the items were body parts. I did not think they were human but was not completely certain. I took photos, collected the items, and met with Texas Parks & Wildlife Game Warden Ray Spears who advised the items might be from a bear. Game Wardens later verified the items as being of a black bear possibly from New Mexico.[48]

The wide variety of activities on campus brings the UPD officer into contact with persons who are not normally part of the university. The opportunity adds to the ability of the officers to keep up ties with the community and local law enforcement. UPD officers play an integral role in welcoming the public to the campus, thereby also making the university more a part of the community.

### The University of Texas at Austin:

UT-Austin is a large school with over 50,000 students and 20,000 employees. The school has a main campus and several off-site locations that the University Police are responsible for covering. These sites include the Pickle Research Center, the Wildflower Center, the Dell Medical Research Center, Paisano Ranch, administrative office buildings downtown, and a site in Port Aransas, which is several hours away.[49] This amounts to roughly 2,000 acres of land and the buildings on the land that require police protection.[50]

In addition to the large area requiring coverage, over 2,400 special events occur on campus each year. The University Police Department employs a full-time lieutenant to coordinate coverage for these activities.[51]

Robert Dahlstrom is chief of police for UT-Austin, a position he has held since 2006. He is the fourth chief at this agency. Prior to taking this position he spent 28 years with the Austin Police Department, retiring as Chief of Staff.[52]

The UT-Austin Police Department (UTPD) employs 65 commissioned officers, 60 guard personnel, and 17 civilian support persons.[53] Their work is much the same as that at Angelo State and Sul Ross, just on a larger scale. There may be over 100,000 persons attending a home football game at UT Austin, while Sul Ross or Angelo State may be lucky to get 1,000 people at their games. Sul Ross might have two officers at a game and one of them will float off to answer other calls.[54] UT Austin will have over 200 officers at their games.[55]

One unique aspect of the UTPD is that they have an officer who works with the FBI's Joint Terrorism Task Force. This officer will interact and train with agents from the FBI and other policing agencies as a joint effort to prevent terrorist attacks in the local Austin area. This situation arose in the aftermath of the 9-11 attacks and provides the UTPD a method of participating in and keeping up with threats to the area since the University would feel the affects of any attack.[56] Smaller schools and those in remote areas such as Sul Ross may not have the opportunity to participate in task forces such as these.

As Dahlstrom[57] puts it, "Campus Law Enforcement is not 'security.' The safety factors are no less than municipal, county or state. I worked municipal for 29 years. UTPD officers stop the same suspects, in the same dark places at the same times as municipal. The threat is no less. Campus officers have received the same training as any other officer and oftentimes more training. They are very proficient with the job that they do and are very professional and well trained."

## School Violence

On April 16, 2007, a lone shooter at Virginia Tech killed 32 people and then himself. The shooting spree began in a dormitory and originally appeared to be a domestic incident. The spree ended two hours later in a classroom across campus.[58] This represents the most deadly campus shooting in history.[59]

The second most deadly occurred in Texas on the UT-Austin campus. On August 1, 1966, Charles Whitman shot his rifle from the tower at the center of campus and killed 16 people. Another 31 were wounded.[60] While this happened 40 years ago, it is still indicative of the need for secure campuses. This shooting was in fact the impetus for creating the University Police Department at UT-Austin.[61]

The UT-Austin campus experienced another shooting episode on September 28, 2010, when student Colton Tooley opened fire with an AK-47. Tooley subsequently killed himself. No other persons were injured.[62]

Response at the school included sirens, loudspeaker warnings, and massive police presence, including officers from departments beyond the UTPD. The campus closed, classes were canceled, and a massive search undertaken in case a second shooter existed. Tooley was, however, alone.[63]

More recently, in the wake of school shootings like these, campus police have had a public spotlight focused on them like never before. This attention ignores the fact that campus crime was decreasing by 9 percent for violent crimes and 30 percent for property crime in a ten-year span from 1994 to 2004.[64]

School violence is changing the role of campus police. In 2008, 13 students died in shootings on college campuses across the United States, an increase over the average of 4 students killed each year from 2000–2004.[65]

Police officers at colleges and universities are increasingly involved in training for violent incidents. Active shooter training, emergency response training, and incident command training are becoming more common, and even required by departments. The training changes the way campus police approach incidents. No longer will officers wait to receive intelligence or backup. Now an officer will go directly into a situation, find the person who is a threat and immobilize that threat, even if it means shooting the person.[66]

According to Dahlstrom,[67] "We were training heavily towards armed subjects before this happened. Since this happened we have improved our campus communication systems 10-fold to get messages out to the campus. We also have bought some tactical equipment for our officers that we did not have previously. We continue to train with surrounding agencies, as we know it would be a multi agency approach to any situation like this. We are full fledged in NIMS [National Incident Management System] compliance so if we have an incident we would handle it properly. VT has brought this type situation to the fore front and all are aware that it is a matter of when, not if."

While training in the areas of active shooter may cause the university police officer to be more prepared, it may also cause the officer to be less inclined toward the traditional role of watchman and order maintainer. This will be something to keep an eye on in the future.

## Crime Reporting

Crime control efforts on campuses resemble those anywhere else in policing. There are, however, some special requirements that apply to campus police departments that are not part of the duties for other law enforcement agencies.

One special requirement relates to the Clery Act, also referred to as the "Crime Awareness and Campus Security Act of 1990." The act's name comes from a student from Lehigh University, Jeanne Clery. Jeanne was raped and murdered in her dorm room on April 15, 1986.[68]

Jeanne's parents discovered that students on the Lehigh campus did not receive information about the 38 violent crimes that had occurred on campus in the three years prior to the murder. The Clerys and other families of crime victims on campuses gathered together to push for a law that would require colleges and universities to make crime statistics more available to students and the public.[69]

The Clery Act requires campuses to publish annual crime reports. Campus police departments are also required to publish warnings about current crime threats, and to publish a crime log. Additionally, information about registered sex offenders who are on campus must be available to the public.[70]

While the Clery Act aims to better inform the public about campus crimes, university police are also involved in efforts to limit the amount of violence occurring on their campuses. In the Texas State University System, an audit of emergency plans on campuses is ongoing. All schools in the system are being required to update this plan.

## Conclusion

Campus police officers play an important role in keeping order on and around college campuses. In the aftermath of school shootings like the one at Virginia Tech in 2007, campus police forces are even more important than ever before. Controversy and "hind-sight" still haunt the Virginia Tech campus police and those who were on campus the day of the shootings.

With campus police more visible, when an incident happens, it does not take long for the police to arrive. Statistics show that crimes on campus are mainly student related.[71] Campus police admit that there is little they can do if students let unknown individuals into the locked dorm buildings. Students need to be more proactive in keeping themselves safe in conjunction with measures taken by campus police.

Overall, with the spotlight on school shootings and other forms of violence on campuses, university police are here to stay. They are more prepared then ever before to tackle these situations and to help keep faculty and students safe.

San Angelo Fire Marshal Don Vardeman.

*Photo Courtesy of Don Vardeman.*

# Chapter 9

# Fire Marshal

## Introduction

Fire can leave significant damage in its wake, including property damage, environmental devastation, and even death. There are many causes of fires including accidents, weather-related causes like lightning, faulty wiring, etc. When a fire is set deliberately or occurs due to negligence, police treat it as a crime of arson. Arson is the second leading cause of death in residential fires and is responsible for 500 deaths every year nationwide. Property damage from arson is estimated to cost $900 million each year.[1]

Arson has always been a crime, but in 1978 it was elevated to the status of Index Crime. In 1982 Congress passed the Anti-Arson Act, which made the crime of arson a permanent part of the Uniform Crime Reports Part I offenses.[2] Basically, this piece of legislation reaffirmed that arson is worthy of being an Index Crime.

Other crimes may also fit within the definition of fire-related. These include insurance fraud and crimes where a fire is set to cover up another crime. The most common reason for arson is in fact financial difficulties.[3] Homicide and burglaries are also crimes that frequently relate to fires.[4]

Due to the seriousness of fires and fire-related crimes, it is necessary for law enforcement and fire personnel to specialize in this area. The best combination of specialization has proven to be an officer who combines law enforcement and fire skills. This is where the fire marshal comes in.

## History of the Position

Seventeen different state-level fire marshal offices existed in the United States in 2004. These offices are separate from the more familiar fire departments. These offices employed 454 full-time sworn officers.[5] In Texas, the State Fire Marshal's Office (SFMO) operates through the Texas Department of Insurance and employs 16 officers including four K-9 Investigators.[6]

The State Fire Marshal's Office began in 1910. Originally, the Commissioner of Insurance or a member of the State Board of Insurance filled this position. In 1975, the state legislature passed a law requiring the State Fire Marshal to be a commissioned peace officer. The State Fire Marshal's Office became a part of the Texas Department of Insurance on September 1, 1997.[7]

Through the years, the state legislature has added official duties to the State Fire Marshal's Office by passing a variety of laws aimed at fire prevention, safety, or regulation. In 1917, fire/arson investigative authority and fire safety authority came under their purview. The Texas Fire Escape Law passed in 1923. Fireworks regulation came about in 1957. In 1969, the Flammable Liquids Law and the Fire Extinguisher Law both passed. Fire Alarm laws passed in 1975 and in 1983, Automatic Fire Sprinkler laws and Smoke Detectors in Hotels laws passed. Fire prevention education became an official duty in 1985. Most recently, a Fire Department Emergency Board emerged in 1989.[8] Each of these laws created a new duty for the SFMO. Sometimes this means inspections or monitoring, and sometimes this means enforcement.

## Modern Fire Marshals

Fire marshals are responsible for conducting arson investigations, undertaking fire inspections, and enforcing fire codes. They may hold employment with local or county agencies or by the Texas State Fire Marshal's Office. Regardless of position, all fire marshals are certified fire/arson investigators, and licensed peace officers.[9]

Fire marshals may also be involved in licensing or monitoring companies in the business of providing fire protection equipment. This may include sprinkler systems, alarms, fire extinguishers, and other equipment.[10] Monitoring of companies who install fire equipment can mean signing off on proper installation so a building can be occupied.

State Fire Marshal investigators are often involved in Fire Safety Inspection Services for public and private buildings. Buildings owned by the state, or housing elderly care, daycare or other dependent care, foster homes, hospitals, and universities or colleges are all subject to Fire Safety Inspections. As a follow up, the State Fire Marshal's Office will also conduct the inspection after a fire in any of these buildings.[11]

## Qualifications to be a Fire Marshal

Like many jobs in law enforcement, a fire marshal's position requirements may vary slightly by department. The following is a list of requirements for fire marshal in Fort Bend County:

- High school diploma or GED
- 1 year job related experience
- TCLEOSE basic peace officer certification
- Texas Commission on Fire Protection Basic Arson Investigator certification
- Texas Commission on Fire Protection Basic Fire Inspector certification
- Computer, verbal and written skills
- Interpersonal skills, ability to work with the public, other employees, and elected officials[12]

These requirements can be taken as representative of the requirements in departments across the state.

## Special Requirements

In addition to meeting the requirements for peace officer certification, fire marshals must meet Texas Commission on Fire Protection (TCFP) certification requirements. Basic certification for Fire Suppression involves a 468-hour course of study. This certification is the very beginning of the levels or specializations that can be achieved.[13]

TCFP certifications exist in the areas of Structure Fire Protection, Aircraft Fire Protection, Marine Fire Protection, Fire Inspector, Arson Investigator, Fire Investigator, Fire Service Instructor, Fire Officer, Hazardous Materials Technician, and Driver/Operator-Pumper. Many of these certifications build on each other. Most also have four levels, based on years of service and advanced training in the area.[14]

## Role of the Fire Marshal

Investigators with the State Fire Marshals office have statewide jurisdiction. They can execute search and arrest warrants and may assist smaller communities who lack their own fire marshal. State Fire Marshal Investigators also have subpoena power without involving a grand jury.[15]

These investigators may investigate any fire in the state of Texas. They will specifically investigate fires resulting in firefighter fatalities. Most investigations involve fire-related crimes like insurance fraud, arson, or homicide; however, there are also some cases where the suspect is a firefighter or law enforcement officer.[16]

Among their other duties, in Travis County the fire marshal's office provides support for the 13 fire departments of the county. They also work with the county's Hazardous Materials Task Force. Additionally they investigate citizen complaints about fire and life safety hazards.[17] Many county level or city level fire marshal offices will engage in similar activities depending on the location.

In smaller locations, the fire marshal position combines with positions such as building inspector. In the city of Andrews, for instance, the two positions have combined almost steadily since the 1960s. In addition to combining positions, more than one county sheriff's office holds a contract as fire marshal.[18] The fire marshal wears a variety of hats in this community; however, they all seem to mesh in a way that provides the city with the services they are looking for.

## Current Duties

San Angelo Fire Marshal's Office:
The San Angelo Fire Marshal's office began operation in 1960 with three officers. As of 2009, there are still only three officers out of eight employees. Current employees include three arson investigators, fire inspectors, and a dangerous building inspector.[19]

The three investigators of the San Angelo Fire Marshal's office rotate duty, being on call 24 hours a day for a week at a time, every three weeks. Their normal shift is 8:00–5:00 Monday through Friday. If called out during other hours, they must still cover the regular shift.[20]

Don Vardeman is fire marshal for the City of San Angelo. His career with this department dates back 29 years. As department head, his responsibilities include both administrative chores such as budgeting and enforcement duties.[21] Vardeman holds certification in a variety of areas including firefighter, fire inspector, fire investigator, and fire instructor. He is also a licensed peace officer.[22]

His daily work provides a great variety of duties and experiences:

"One of the reasons I still enjoy this job is no day is the same. We do so many varied things every day it is never boring. In this job you meet and deal with the richest of the rich and the poorest of the poor. Yesterday for example, I ordered the demolition of a burned house, met with four of my employees on various problems, talked with the Mayor three times on problems, checked on billing for a local bar, met with the Assistant City Attorney on filing charges and met with 60+ disgruntled people, the Assistant City Manager and Planning Manger about an apartment complex coming into their neighborhood. I also reviewed an arson case that occurred this weekend with one of my Investigators."[23]

While the 911 system is not directly involved in the work of the fire marshal, it does play a role. Obviously, people can use 911 to report fires or fire-related crimes. Sometimes however these calls are false alarms. In San Angelo, children made many of these false alarms to 911. The fire marshal's office now incorporates a segment on proper use of 911 in their Fire Prevention Week programs at public schools.[24]

## State Fire Marshal's Office:

The State Fire Marshal's Office employs 16 investigators and a variety of support staff. Salary for investigators with the State Fire Marshal's Office ranges from $33,000 to $42,000 per year.[25]

John Kondratick is a Fire/Arson Investigator for the Texas State Fire Marshal's Office, a position he has held for almost four years. His responsibilities include investigating arsons and related crimes. Mostly this means writing reports, filling out paperwork, and following up on leads in his active investigations.[26] Occasionally, there is more action: "A few years ago in Van Horn, suspect enters a business and pours an unidentified liquid throughout the building in an attempt to burn it down. The suspect used the bathroom and flushed the toilet. The water pipe leaked and a passerby who used to work at the business saw the water leaking and knew no one should be in the building outside business hours. Passersby called Sheriff's Office and the suspect was arrested."[27]

State Fire Marshal investigators do not routinely respond to calls for service in the way other law enforcement agencies might. However, "911 assists us greatly if a dispatcher can obtain information regarding a possible suspect fleeing a scene or can obtain information of where and how a fire is spreading. That helps us in our investigation."[28]

Many smaller communities do not have a fire marshal of their own. An investigator from the State Fire Marshal's Office can fulfill this role when needed. Working well with other agencies is therefore necessary in fire marshal cases if they are to provide assistance or if they expect to get assistance when conducting investigations.[29]

In fiscal year 2009, there were 10 fires reported at college campuses across the state of Texas. The State Fire Marshal's Office investigated each one. Only two of these fires qualified as possible arson. More likely, they were negligence, as were several of the other fires. During this same period, the State Fire Marshal's Office investigated a fire at the Estelle Unit of the Texas Department of Criminal Justice. The cause of this fire is undetermined.[30]

Investigators will also conduct an investigation for all firefighter fatalities that occur in the state. Since September of 2001, there have been 26 such fatalities. Five were the result of vehicular crashes where the firefighter was not wearing a seatbelt. Investigators determined that four of the five probably would not have died if they had worn a seatbelt. The State Fire Marshal's Office now promotes a seatbelt pledge for all firefighters across the state.[31]

Public Education:

Fire marshals' offices at all levels engage in a variety of public education programs that are designed to heighten awareness of the dangers of fire, and to help persons be prepared for what to do in case of fire. These programs range in scope from those aimed at school children to those aimed at entire communities or the entire state.

The State Fire Marshal's Office sponsors several statewide initiatives to draw attention to specific types of fire dangers. On such program is Arson

Awareness Week, which normally runs through the first week of May. This program focuses on the threat from arson for profit-type crimes.[32]

Another program offered through the State Fire Marshal's Office is Burn Awareness week. This program focuses on preventing injuries related to gasoline burns. In particular, children in the early teen years are at risk for this type of injury. The program involves parents, teachers, and other groups in the prevention effort.[33]

A third program that runs through the State Fire Marshal's Office is "Have an Exit Strategy." This program promotes safety in public buildings by encouraging citizens to be aware of their surroundings and to locate alternative exits when in a public building.[34]

The State Fire Marshal's Office provides many free resources to educational institutions and other public groups in order to help promote fire safety. Many of the free resources will be in the form of written material for handing out. There are also curriculum materials and videos to help teachers and leaders prepare lessons on fire safety.[35]

County and city-level fire marshals will also engage in public education, but on a smaller scale. Normally this means giving presentations to local schools and civic groups. In San Angelo, much of the public education provided by the fire marshal involves Fire Prevention Week programs at local schools.

## Conclusion

Estimates show that one in four domestic fires is the result of arson. The volume of crimes relating to fire requires a special agency devoted to them.[36] The fire marshal is that specialist. Fire marshals represent a combination of peace officer and fire fighter. Through investigations, licensing, and public education, the fire marshal's goal is to keep the public safe from fires and fire-related crimes.

Inspectors from the State Fire Marshal's Office have statewide jurisdiction with the ability to issue subpoenas without involving the grand jury. Their role in investigating fires in public buildings and state-run facilities ensures the safest situations possible for persons using these buildings.

The position of fire marshal is increasingly important in today's society to handle the fire related issues that happen in our every day life. The special skills these officers bring to the job cannot be replicated in other forms of law enforcement and therefore remain in demand in our society.

San Angelo Deputy City Marshal Brian Albertson.

*Photo taken by Lorie Rubenser.*

# Chapter 10

# City Marshal

## Introduction

The city marshal position is one of the oldest forms of paid municipal police service in the United States. This position was traditionally the only law enforcement within the city and was thus directly responsive to the needs of the city. Other law enforcement belonged to the county or territory and only occasionally helped in the city.

The position of city marshal has evolved in many cities to become the municipal police chief. There are, however still 316 city marshals remaining in Texas,[1] some in cities with large police departments.

## History of the Position

In 1823, Boston became the first city in the United States to appoint a city marshal. The appointment was the culmination of moves by the city council to address rapid population growth, the insufficiencies of the watch system and the incorporation of the city. Benjamin Pollard became the first city marshal. He was appointed by and reported directly to the mayor.[2]

In addition to law enforcement, Pollard acted as health officer, licensed dogs, coordinated fire brigades, and planned parades. Law enforcement was often secondary, but included arresting of poachers from Boston Common, and prosecuting of his own cases.[3]

In 1848, Boston created a separate day watch, which immediately clashed with the pre-existing night watch. The city marshal had to referee these conflicts in addition to conducting his normal duties. Finally, in 1854 the city reorganized its municipal services to include a police department that would be under the control of a chief. The city marshal position transformed into the police chief position.[4]

## City Marshals in Texas

On July 26, 1880, the city of El Paso appointed its first city marshal, John B. Tays. Tays was already famous for being the only Texas Ranger in history to surrender his forces.[5] On August 3 of the same year, the city added an assistant city marshal. Neither man had an official salary; therefore both held regular jobs in addition to their law enforcement positions.

In addition to law enforcement duties, the city marshal maintained the roads in and around the city. This in itself was a full-time job in a city with little real sanitation and predominantly packed-dirt roads. Floods, garbage dumping, and constant overuse turned many roads into mud bogs several feet deep.[6]

The city council fired Tays and his assistant on October 25, 1880. The next city marshal did even worse, lasting only a month. A series of men were then appointed and fired from the position until Dallas Stoudenmire was appointed on April 11, 1881.[7]

Stoudenmire had been a former army man and former Texas Ranger. The man he assumed the job from, William Johnson, was so upset that he became drunk and attempted to kill Stoudenmire in a gunfight a week later. Stoudenmire easily won the gun battle, but gained a reputation for fighting.[8]

In addition to law enforcement, Stoudenmire kept the jail, maintained the streets, enforced local ordinances, collected fines, occasionally collected taxes, policed the city's opium dens, and controlled the population of loose dogs by shooting them. In order to accomplish all of this work, Stoudenmire was able to convince the city to pay him a full-time salary and to pay his deputies. He was also able to keep a portion of the fines he collected in order to supplement his low salary.[9]

Stoudenmire was frequently drunk, engaged in street fights, killed several people, and had many feuds with the local Texas Rangers. He was, however, highly progressive in his law enforcement duties. He insisted that his men wear uniforms. He personally raised the money and purchased badges for them. He also convinced the city to buy new jail cells that were more secure than the existing facilities.[10]

Stoudenmire engaged in ongoing disputes with many of the disreputable persons in the city. On September 18, 1882, he had his final disagreement with them and was killed in an ambush on the city streets.[11]

From this questionable beginning, city marshals in Texas advanced through more auspicious times, sometimes being involved in famous cases like the Great Northern Express train robbery of 1901. Orland Camillo Hanks robbed the train on July 3, 1901, as it traveled from Washington State to Helena, Montana. He escaped with $40,000 and traveled to Texas. City Marshal Taylor of San Antonio subsequently attempted to arrest him in early April of 1902. When Hanks resisted he was shot and killed by Taylor and his deputies.[12]

City marshals in Texas also moved toward professionalism during this period. In 1898, the City Marshals and Chiefs of Police Union began in Texas. The annual meeting of the union provided opportunities for discussion of common policing issues and solutions among the members. In the 1934 meeting, for example, discussion focused on access to police radio frequencies by civilians. The members present expressed unanimous disapproval of both the creation and accessibility of radios that would allow private citizens to listen to police radio frequencies.[13]

Other issues of concern at the 1934 meeting were the relationship between kidnapping and racketeering. Discussion also included fingerprinting and police marksmanship. These issues represent a continuing concern with technology and its use by police. Fingerprinting in particular represented a continuing issue remaining from the 1928 meeting.[14] Police use of automobiles, airplanes, and machine guns also received mention in 1928 as part of the discussion of the need for police to keep up technologically with criminals.

As cities grew, their law enforcement needs expanded exponentially. For most cities, the answer was to create a municipal police department. El Paso, for example, made this transition in 1884.[15]

Most cities making the transition from city marshal to police department simply re-titled the existing personnel: the city marshal became the police chief. The title "City Marshal" in fact normally ceased to exist when this transition occurred.

## Modern City Marshals

Modern city marshals have moved away from running police departments, shooting stray dogs, and keeping streets clean. Today's city marshal is a highly professional law enforcement officer who concentrates on a few specialized areas. Most of the work city marshals now do relates to warrants and other court duties. This means their time centers on court sessions and the hours in which they can find wanted persons. In this regard, city marshals are very much like constables.

Very little of the city marshal's work is in direct response to a citizen complaint. Law-abiding citizens may in fact never encounter a city marshal.

## Qualifications to be a City Marshal

The general requirements to become a city marshal in Texas are the same as for any other law enforcement position. The candidate must have met the licensing requirements set out by the Texas Commission on Law Enforcement Officer Standards and Education as laid out in Chapter 2.

Some cities will require applicants to meet additional criteria. Candidates in Fort Worth, for example, must have two years' prior experience in law enforcement. Additionally the candidate will be required to pass a drug test and certify that they have not used illegal drugs for at least five years. An alcohol test may also be required. Standard background checks, prior employment verification, driving record checks, etc. will also be performed.[16]

## Special Requirements

There is no special training or licensing required by the state of Texas for persons holding a city marshal or deputy city marshal position. Individual departments may, however, have requirements. These individualized requirements tend to relate to computer systems, reporting systems, and the like. Individual departments may or may not have formal on-the-job training for new hires.[17]

## Role of the City Marshal

While many cities did away with their city marshal's office when they created a municipal police department, a new trend is bringing back the city marshal.

Both Baytown and San Antonio have opened city marshal offices: Baytown in 2004,[18] and San Antonio in 2007.[19]

City marshals are often involved in warrant service for the courts. These warrants cover anything from outstanding traffic tickets to criminal violations.

In 2007, a Great Texas Warrant Roundup occurred. In San Angelo this program operates through the city marshal's office in conjunction with other local area law enforcement, including city, county, and even university officers.[20]

In February of 2009, the *San Angelo Standard Times*[21] printed the names of persons in the San Angelo area who had outstanding warrants. These persons had until March 6 to take care of their warrants. After this deadline, any persons with remaining warrants were subject to arrest and jailing. No one arrested during this program received a personal recognizance bond. The article listed 7,000 names.

In the course of the Warrant Roundup, 225 agencies signed up to participate. Statewide, officers cleared over 204,000 warrants. In San Angelo alone, the municipal court cleared 4,102 warrants. The court collected $262,768 in court costs, fees, bonds, and fines.[22]

The Great Texas Warrant Roundup is a fine example of cooperative efforts among law enforcement agencies across the state of Texas. It also demonstrates the effectiveness of the city marshal's office in San Angelo when it comes to finding persons with outstanding warrants.

## Current Duties

### San Angelo:

The San Angelo City Marshal's Office is comprised of six deputy marshals, one city marshal and a chief marshal. Starting salaries range in the mid $30,000s.[23] The office also employs roughly 20 clerks/civilians.[24]

The city marshal's office is directly responsive to two municipal judges in San Angelo.[25] Hiring decisions go through Municipal Judge Gilbert. The chief marshal will do the interview and background. The desired candidate's application goes to the judge who has final say.[26]

Brian Albertson is a deputy city marshal with the San Angelo Municipal Court. He has been with the San Angelo City Marshal's Office for four years.

Before taking the position in San Angelo, Albertson was a deputy sheriff in Coke County.[27]

A typical day at the office includes making a list of contacts for warrants service. This means the marshal will go to homes and places of employment, trying to serve warrants. City marshals have statewide jurisdiction to serve city warrants.[28]

The city marshal will spend a large amount of time traveling around the city to serve warrants. Paperwork occupies the bulk of time.

The San Angelo City Marshal, through municipal court, reinforces the Texas Juvenile Truant program. If a public school student misses a certain number of school days, the municipal court judge sentences the student to a designated program where the student will engage in community service activities. The city marshal monitors the site to make sure that the student fulfills the sentence.[29]

Johanna Nunez also works for the city marshal's office in San Angelo. She has spent the last three years of her 15-year career with this office as juvenile case manager. In this position, Nunez is responsible for truancy cases within the city limits.[30]

As the juvenile case manager, Nunez responds to all charges of truancy by entering citations and by preparing charges for the court docket. She continues her work by acting as bailiff for truancy and juvenile court cases.[31]

Once a juvenile's case has been through court, Nunez continues to work with the cases by ensuring the juvenile complies with the court order. If a student is not sentenced to a specific program, but rather a term of community service, Nunez can help them secure community service opportunities. She can also offer courses or other programs to meet their sentence requirements.[32]

Enforcing warrants and dealing with truancy are important functions in any community. The efforts of the city marshal in San Angelo serve not just to enforce rules, but also to encourage responsibility and to deter undesirable behaviors.

## San Antonio:

In San Antonio, the city marshal's office recently re-opened in response to the large number of outstanding warrants in the city. The city marshal's office in San Antonio employs one city marshal, two deputies, and a support staff.

Their workload is composed entirely of outstanding misdemeanor warrants from the municipal court.[33]

The municipal court deals only with Class C Misdemeanor cases and signs roughly 130,000 warrants for outstanding cases each year. The city marshal's office will attempt to contact persons by telephone to give them the opportunity to clear the warrant. People who fail to do so will be arrested.[34]

Currently only adjudicated cases involving persons who appeared in court, agreed to pay a fine, and then failed to actually pay, go to the city marshal's office. Plans exist to add two more deputies and expand the type of cases that will be handled.[35]

## Conclusion

City marshals were an exciting part of law enforcement in the old West. As cities grew, however, the city marshal position often translated into a police chief with all the responsibilities of a municipal police department.

Today, city marshals are again playing an important role in law enforcement. Not only are they responsible for municipal court security, but they also write tickets and serve warrants. City marshals may also enforce truancy regulations in communities where this is a problem.

City marshals and constables perform many of the same duties, but within different jurisdictions. Constables are elected officials who perform their duties in the county where elected. City marshals obtain employment through regular channels and perform their duties within city limits. The combined city/county coverage provided by city marshals and constables ensures the full reach of the courts.

It is safe to say that city marshals are becoming more popular in the law enforcement theatre. Municipal courts are seeing a need for enhanced abilities to enforce warrants. In many communities, the answer is to re-create the city marshal position. As society expands, the city marshal will see his role expand to include monitoring truancy and supporting other law enforcement agencies.

TABC Officer Matt West in front of a still after it was destroyed by using a pick axe.

*Photo Courtesy of Matt West.*

# Chapter 11
# Texas Alcoholic Beverage Commission

## Introduction

Brewing beer and making hard alcohol has occurred in this country from almost the moment of European settlement. Each industry has followed its own path of development, followed closely by attempts to control almost all aspects. Government control focuses mostly on taxation and regulation of sales.[1]

The American experience with alcohol has been controversial for much of our history, culminating in a period of Prohibition. The 18th Amendment, passed in 1919, banned the "manufacture, sale, or transportation . . ." of alcohol. Prohibition lasted 13 years and was ultimately a failure. The 21st Amendment ended Prohibition in 1933.[2]

The end of Prohibition did not signal an end to the issues surrounding the alcohol industry, however. The controversy over the proper role of alcohol continues, with groups like Mothers Against Drunk Driving (MADD) attempting to bring to light the bad side of alcohol usage. Drunk driving, public intoxication, and other offenses are violations of the law, which most law enforcement agencies may address.

There is more to the alcohol industry than just what the drinkers are doing while under the influence. As an industry, there are taxes to be paid. There are laws regulating who can purchase alcohol, specifically only persons who are 21 years of age. There are also laws dictating who may sell alcohol and where sales may occur. These laws may include restrictions on the type of alcohol. All aspects of the alcohol industry require some level of regulation.

## History of the Position

As of 2004, there were 17 specialized policing agencies in the United States dedicated to alcohol-law enforcement. These agencies employ 1,219 full-time sworn personnel.[3] In Texas, the Texas Alcoholic Beverage Commission (TABC) represents this type of agency.

TABC came into being in 1935, two years after the end of Prohibition. Regulatory powers cover all facets of the industry from manufacture through transportation, importation, sales, taxes, and advertising.[4]

In the history of TABC, only two agents have died in the line of duty. The first was Delbert H. Pearson. On January 18, 1973, a suspect shot Pearson at close range with a 12-gauge shotgun while subject to a stake-out of an illegal whiskey stash. The suspect had seven prior arrests with six convictions. He received a sentence of life in prison.[5]

The second TABC agent killed in the line of duty was Joseph Thomas "Jay" Crews. On September 21, 1979, Crews was driving away from a business where he had conducted an inspection when a drunk driver struck him in a head on collision. Crews died instantly.[6] It is ironic that Crews was working for an agency that seeks to prevent drunk driving.

As we can see, compared to most agencies, TABC has a low rate of officer deaths. This is not because the job is without danger, but because TABC consists of highly skilled agents who engage in a large amount of prevention work, and who know how to work with other agencies when needed. The officers still face a risk every time they go work and this risk is not less due to low numbers of line-of-duty deaths.

## Modern TABC

Organizationally, TABC is composed of six divisions, each of which plays a role in regulating the alcohol industry in Texas. Five of the six divisions do not involve law enforcement personnel but rather engage in more administrative functions.[7] These divisions include:

- Licensing – issues 100,000 licenses and permits in 60 categories each year
- General Counsel/Legal Services – prosecution of violations, review of protests, response to legal inquiries

## Chapter 11: Texas Alcoholic Beverage Commission

- Compliance – performs audits and ensures taxes and fees are paid, oversees product testing and approves labels
- Ports of Entry – collects taxes and regulates personal imports at the Texas-Mexico border for both alcohol and cigarettes
- Education and Prevention – operates educational programs for the public and sellers, aims to curb underage drinking and driving while intoxicated
- Enforcement Division – sworn peace officers who undertake enforcement duties relating to the alcohol industry[8]

The combination of these six divisions has the ability to reach all aspects of the liquor industry.

The Enforcement Division is TABC's largest unit. There are 300 agents in this unit, each having statewide jurisdiction. Salaries range from $38,199 as an agent trainee to $57,733 for an agent with 20 or more years of service. Sergeant, lieutenant, and captain positions are also available with pay varying by years of service.[9]

Enforcement agents hold assignments around the state at both major offices and smaller outposts. Outposts are generally in rural areas and may cover several counties. There are normally fewer than five agents at these outposts so each officer has a lot of ground to cover.[10]

Each year TABC agents inspect over 72,000 businesses that hold licenses to sell alcohol. Agents also visit roughly 70 percent of the licensed businesses throughout the state. The process allows for more open communication on matters of concern to both sides.[11]

During the inspections, agents are looking for the following:

- Licenses and required signs must be properly posted
- Marketing and promotional materials must meet requirements
- Customers must not be intoxicated or under age
- Sales of alcohol must be confined to types authorized by the license or permit
- A proper invoice must exist for all alcohol bought and sold
- No other violations of state law may exist[12]

Fewer than 15 percent of inspections reveal violations. Most of these violations are minor and result in a warning rather than sanctions. Businesses with licenses to sell alcohol appear to be doing a good job of self-policing.[13]

## Qualifications to be a TABC Officer

Agents within the Enforcement Division of TABC must be licensed peace officers who have met the criteria set out by the TCLEOSE. Additional requirements include being in good physical condition with no disabilities that would interfere with the job. Agents must have uncorrected vision of no worse than 20/200 or corrected vision of no worse than 20/30 and must not be colorblind. An extensive background check occurs before employment. Credit history, past employment, and driving record checks will be included in the background check.[14]

TABC will also hold a commission for agents who have retired from the agency. The commission allows a retired person to hold the title of "Special Agent" or "Representative." A person applying for this commission must be qualified to be a peace officer under the rules set forth by the TCLEOSE. The applicant must also certify that they are not involved in any business within the alcoholic beverage industry.[15]

Retired agents who maintain a commission with TABC have limits placed on their use of police powers. Agents may not engage in active enforcement of any laws not directly necessary to preserve life under normal circumstances. Special agents or representatives may, however, be called to duty by TABC or the governor in cases of emergency. In such cases the agent returns to full duty.[16]

Special agents or representatives may become involved in private security, guard work, or investigative work with some limitations.[17] The special agent is thus able to work part-time and keep busy in retirement. TABC benefits by having a cadre of former officers available if needed.

## Special Requirements

New agents with TABC must complete the TABC basic academy training, even if already licensed as a peace officer. After completion of the academy, the agent trainee will complete a 12-month probationary period. During this period, the agent trainee will take part in a field-training program. Field training consists of 18 weeks of on-the-job training. Written exams and evaluations will determine the trainee's progress. If at any point the trainee fails a test or evaluation, remedial training is mandatory. Three failures of the same test may result in termination of employment.[18]

## Role of TABC

TABC officers engage in a variety of duties relating to alcohol, including enforcement, public education, and inspections of licensed establishments. They also engage in a variety of investigative/enforcement activities that on the surface do not appear related to alcohol. These cases may include those relating to prostitution, gambling, narcotics trafficking, illegal weapons, and organized crime.[19]

In addition to handling their own law enforcement activities, TABC officers may assist other policing agencies when needed. In 2008, TABC agents assisted DPS and other agencies in responding to Hurricane Ike.

Following the storm, TABC agents assisted by enforcing the curfews, enforcing roadblocks, patrolling the neighborhoods, and checking for suspicious activity. The goal was to deter scavengers and prevent looters from breaking into homes and businesses or stealing downed power lines for their copper. TABC assisted the Texas Department of Public Safety with an escort of a large convoy of 18-wheelers carrying emergency supplies, ice, water, and MREs (Meals Ready to Eat), to a distribution point. Agents also assisted the Texas Department of Public Safety with an escort of a convoy of trucks to a fuel distribution center. TABC agents have assisted with crowd control and traffic direction at points of distribution; crowd control at gas stations and grocery stores; providing security services for hospitals; and traffic control, ensuring that only residents, approved contractors and clean-up crews were allowed into affected areas.[20]

## Current Duties

Shuddell Lindsey has been a law enforcement agent for TABC for three years. Before this, he was a police sergeant with the Lexington Police Department. In his position as sergeant he worked with TABC agents on a variety of programs.[21]

Lindsey works at the TABC Outpost Office in San Angelo. During a normal week, he works three overnight shifts where enforcement duties are a priority. One day a week is devoted to day-shift work including public education and court hearings.[22]

According to Lindsey,[23] the TABC agent can be described as a combination of detective, health inspector, and patrol officer. No day is the same as the next, but on average Lindsey will arrest somewhere between 2 and 12 people each week. Much of the difference in arrest rate depends on how many special events or large-scale investigations occur during that week. A TABC agent in a larger city like Austin can expect to make more arrests.

Law enforcement duties include inspections, investigations, and sting operations. Agents may also assist other law enforcement agencies. Many of these duties occur at night and involve long hours.[24] The individual agent has a lot of discretion in setting work hours in order to be most effective.[25]

Inspections average around 30 minutes per business, depending on the number of violations. Several inspections can occur each week, with more occurring in the larger cities like Houston and Dallas.[26]

Investigations can involve a variety of crimes relating to alcohol or taking place in businesses licensed to sell alcohol. On average TABC agents will conduct at least one investigation per week, again with more occurring in the larger cities. If the investigation concerns a major crime like a murder in a bar, the agent may spend all of their time on the one investigation until it is complete. Big investigations could take two weeks or more of undivided attention.[27]

Another type of investigation conducted by TABC agents is a "source investigation." Serious automobile accidents involving alcohol or DWI cases may become the subject of this kind of investigation to determine where the alcohol came from. The goal is to determine if the source of the alcohol was acting legally when providing the alcohol to the persons involved in the case. Filing of charges against sources that were not acting within the law occurs frequently.[28]

At least three times a month, the TABC agent will engage in operations designed to deter underage drinking. Operations include stings and programs such as Cops in Shops and Operation Fake Out.[29]

Sting operations by TABC often catch retail sales of alcohol to minors. Originally, stings occurred in stores where patrons purchased alcohol for consumption at another site. In 1995, use of stings expanded to include places where drinking alcohol occurs on site.[30]

In a sting operation, the TABC agent uses a minor, normally 16 to 18 years of age, who attempts to purchase alcohol. If the minor succeeds, agents arrest the seller. Rates of sales to minors during sting operations have fallen from 35 percent to 20 percent in recent years.[31]

### Chapter 11: Texas Alcoholic Beverage Commission

Cops in Shops is a cooperative operation where TABC agents go to a retailer's location and pose as customers or as employees. The agent is then in a position to arrest minors who attempt to purchase alcohol. The agent has the opportunity to educate the retail employees on ways to spot fake IDs, intoxicated persons, and other problems. Retailers may request to participate in this program to enhance their own efforts to curb sales to minors.[32]

Operation Fake Out targets underage drinking at bars and other similar locations. TABC agents position themselves inside the door to conduct a second review of IDs after the door attendant has passed people through. The TABC agent will use magnetic strip readers and ultraviolet lights to detect fake IDs.[33]

Agents arrest any persons caught with fake IDs. An interrogation may occur in order to find information on the source of the fake ID. TABC forwards any information gathered from the interrogation to DPS or the Secret Service for follow up.[34] Conceivably, a TABC Fake Out arrest could break up a fake ID production operation that would sell fake IDs to terrorists.

TABC agents may assist other law enforcement agencies during special events like concerts, festivals, and other group attractions. During these events, alcohol enforcement is only part of the picture. TABC agents will assist with crowd control and order maintenance. Bicycle patrols are an increasingly common method for TABC to deliver this service.[35]

In San Angelo, special events like concerts occur roughly twice a month, with more outdoor events in the summer. Each of these events occupies around four hours of the agent's time. During this time, the agent may issue warrants rather than make arrests. Arrests would halt the operation, as the agent would have to take the arrested person to jail for booking. Warrants indicate that some time in the next 30 days the person is subject to arrest if they do not turn themselves in first.[36]

One day of each week is reserved for public education duties. During these duties, the TABC agent will go to local schools, local military bases, and other locations to teach kids about the dangers of improper use of alcohol. The agent may also go to retail outlets like Wal-Mart to teach employees aspects of the Alcoholic Beverage Code, how to identify a fake ID, and other information to help them stay within the law as they sell alcohol.[37]

In general, TABC agents do not respond to 911 calls. Citizens can make complaints about alcohol violations, however, by filling out a complaint form and submitting it through fax or email. Persons wishing to file a complaint in person may go to the local TABC office if one is available. If enough information exists in the complaint to warrant investigation, an agent takes the case.[38]

Rather than taking reports through 911, TABC maintains a toll-free number for citizens to report underage drinking. The Texas Underage Drinking Hotline number is 1-888-THE-TABC. An average of 56 complaints came to the hotline each month in 2004.[39]

In addition to inspecting licensed retail locations, TABC agents often inspect unlicensed locations where alcohol violation reports have occurred. Underage drinking parties are of particular concern, but other offenses are also subject to intervention. Bootlegging, for instance, is still a crime people commit even with the relative ease of legally acquiring alcohol.[40]

Along with bootlegging, some persons are operating illegal stills to manufacture alcohol. According to former agent Matt West, this manufacture can take some unappetizing forms:

In the summer of 2004, TABC Agent Matthew West busted a moonshine still in Harrison County, TX. The still is known as a "three barrel still" because of the use of three 55 gallon drums used in the distillation process. The barrels were purchased from a local oil company.

"The defendant would place the barrels on a large fire and heat them until they would start to glow red. According to the defendant, this would burn the oil out. He would then rinse them out with lye. After a rinse, he would begin making his 'shine.'

"The end product was observed to have a blue tint to it, much like kerosene. This is probably attributed to the oil residue that slowly leached out of the metal during the cooking process.

"The entire shack that the still was located in had a thick oily film coating everything. The sour mash was kept in an old deep freezer. The seal on the freezer chest allowed the mash to "burp" (allow the gasses to escape from the fermentation process) and then close back again. The smell is literally nauseating."

Up until this bust, there had not been a still busted by TABC in Texas for almost a decade. Between 2004–2009, only two other stills in Texas have been located by TABC.[41]

Other investigations led to the discovery of crimes not commonly associated with liquor law violations: "March 1st, 2005: Eagle Pass, TX: Agents with the Texas Alcoholic Beverage Commission conducted a raid on an illegal cock fight. The original investigation involved selling alcohol without a permit. After conducting surveillance with the assistance of the US Border patrol, it was determined that much illegal activity was going on. Agents arrested several suspects for Organized Criminal Activity, Sale of Alcohol without a Permit, Possession of Cocaine, and Animal Cruelty."[42]

TABC expects its agents to be involved in all aspects of the alcohol industry, but as the previous passages indicate, alcohol is a part of many other crimes. The TABC agent must therefore be prepared to face a variety of strange situations, and to enforce any law on the books as they go about their jobs.

### Homeland Security:

As with most law enforcement agencies across America, 9-11 has had an effect on TABC. For example, the commission has created a more detailed background check system for persons applying for liquor licenses. This helps prevent terrorists from making money in the liquor industry.[43]

TABC has also been able to add 65 law enforcement agents through Homeland Security grants. Specialized Homeland Security agents now aid in the mission of the agency. Other Homeland Security grants have provided new equipment for the agency.[44]

## Conclusion

The Texas Alcoholic Beverage Commission has become an integral part of law enforcement today. In the past, TABC played a minor role in law enforcement, mainly dealing with juvenile sales and liquor establishment guidelines. All of this has changed in modern times. Recently, Homeland Security has helped TABC to expand its operations by funding 65 commissioned officers. In return, operations undertaken by TABC such as Operation Fake Out can help Homeland Security by identifying sources of false identification.[45]

TABC is not without controversy. One controversial program, Operation Last Call, represented a proactive strategy by TABC to reduce drunk driving, but only lasted from 2005 to 2006 due to its aggressive enforcement tactic. TABC agents actively sought individuals displaying characteristics of inebriation in bars, taverns, and other alcohol-serving establishments. Over 2,200 people faced arrest, jail time, and fines. Many complained of over-reach when persons with a designated driver or in other circumstances faced arrest.[46] The operation remains suspended at this time.[47]

TABC officers perform a variety of functions not normally associated with alcohol enforcement. Investigations may include cases involving prostitution, gambling, narcotics, trafficking, illegal weapons, and organized crime.

We have also seen TABC at their best during Hurricane Ike, when officers all over the state joined forces to help stranded residents get to safety. TABC is ultimately a fine example of law enforcement and cooperative efforts to get the job done. This agency will no doubt continue to play an important role in the future of law enforcement.

Tom Green County Bailiff Tonia Jennings.

*Photo Courtesy of Tonia Jennings.*

# Chapter 12
# Bailiffs

## Introduction

Under normal circumstances, the general public may never have a reason to encounter a bailiff. Only persons with business in a courthouse will encounter the bailiff, specifically potential jurors and other persons involved in a court case. Even these people, however, may not fully understand the functions of the bailiff or know that the bailiff is a licensed peace officer.

Modern media has done nothing to promote awareness of this important position, with bailiffs playing minor supporting roles in courtroom dramas. Perhaps the most famous television bailiffs were Bull and Roz on the 1980s sitcom *Night Court*. While entertaining, these two comedic individuals did almost nothing that resembles the real work of the bailiff.

## History of the Position

Like the constable, the bailiff has roots in medieval times. In England, the bailiff served either the lord of the manor or the hundred courts and sheriff. The position was supervisory. Those serving on a manor or estate kept accounts, collected rents and fines, and were responsible for all the land and buildings that made up the estate.[1]

The term bailiwick was originally associated with the work of bailiffs. A bailiwick was the geographical area under the jurisdiction of the bailiff. Modern usage still implies either geographic jurisdiction or an area of responsibility denoted in a non-geographic way.[2]

Bailiffs, called *bailli* in the Norman world, emerged in the Angevin era of the early 1100s. The position was given to a member of the king's administration and was often responsible for holding local court hearings or assizes.[3]

In 1285, bailiffs received specific mention in the Statute of Winchester.[4] This statute created a rudimentary system for handling criminal matters whereby the sheriff was empowered to organize the people in hundreds, use the "hue and cry" system for raising a posse, and hold court to deal with crime matters.[5]

The Statute of Winchester goes on to indicate, "And the bailiffs of towns each week, or at least every fortnight, shall make investigation concerning men lodged in the suburbs or in the outskirts of the towns; and if they find anybody harboring or otherwise lodging persons suspected of being in any respect violators of the peace, the bailiffs shall have justice done in the matter."[6]

Sheriffs assigned bailiffs to serve the courts. The main core of their job was to assist the judge in various tasks including serving process, executing writs, assembling juries, and collecting court fines. All of these duties were essentially order-keeping functions undertaken during the biannual court sessions.[7]

In some areas, the sheriffs actually controlled the county courts whose dockets contained cases concerning debt or small-scale damages. In order to force people to appear for these cases, the sheriff would rely on the bailiff, who in turn would command the petty constable to bring persons to court.[8]

Jury service received no compensation during this time and therefore members of the public often avoided it. The bailiff was responsible for maintaining a list of persons who were freeholders and eligible for service. Bailiffs often asked extra persons to show up just to ensure a full jury could be empanelled.[9]

French bailiffs, or *bailli*, of the thirteen to fifteenth centuries were principal parts of the king's central government. The king appointed the bailiff who then reported directly to him. This situation gave them more power than their English counterparts.[10]

The French bailiff also engaged in a wider variety of duties than his English counterpart did. These duties included supervising lesser officers in the king's government, maintaining public order, calling men for military service, collecting taxes from those who paid their way out of military service, and supervising the local troops. The French bailiff was also in charge of the king's payroll and the royal treasury.[11]

Rather than assisting judges in court, French bailiffs held their own courts, with original jurisdiction over cases involving nobility and appellate jurisdiction over cases coming from local courts. The bailiff court would also hear all cases involving the king's domain and the king's rights.[12]

While choice of bailiff candidates required care to ensure hiring of even-tempered persons, their assistants, underbailiffs or special bailiffs, were often of lower quality. This often created problems with community members and tarnished the image of the job.[13]

With such wide-ranging tasks, the bailiffs of the day proved unable to keep up with their work. Other government positions were created to take away some of the burden. Financial matters transferred to accounting specialists called receivers. Military affairs transferred totally to the military. Lawyers and judges also emerged to take over the work of the bailiff, eventually replacing him entirely in court functions.[14]

The power of the bailiff diminished forever by the seventeenth century. In France, the position still held a lifelong term and was often passed down from father to son, but there was no real power remaining. Bailiffs became nothing more than another person with a title.[15]

## Bailiffs in Texas

There is nothing particularly unique about bailiffs in the state of Texas. History has lost most records demonstrating the early beginnings of the position, but it would be reasonable to assume the bailiff came to Texas in the same way the court system did: communities were in need of some mechanism to promote justice. Since the sheriff was often the only law enforcement officer within a wide area, it was only natural that a deputy held assignment to the court for security.

## Modern Bailiffs

Today the bailiff is an important part of the courtroom work group. The work group is composed of the common actors in the courtroom including the judge, prosecutor, defense attorney, court reporter, and bailiff.[16] Of this group of court functionaries, the bailiff is the only person armed while in the courtroom. They are also the only person whose primary function relates to security.

Generally a bailiff holds a law enforcement commission through the county's sheriff's' office. In many places, they may not have full police powers. Some states allow the bailiff to be a member of the local police department. At the federal court level, the US Marshals Service may assign bailiffs.[17]

## Qualifications to be a Bailiff

First, in the state of Texas a bailiff must meet the criteria to be a licensed peace officer. Chapter 2 covers these criteria in detail. After meeting these criteria, the potential bailiff must meet whatever department-level criteria there may be. As the bailiff normally holds a commission through a sheriff's office, the bailiff may be required to meet the employment criteria set for a deputy sheriff. In fact, in smaller communities, some bailiffs will work part-time in the court and part-time as a deputy.

## Special Requirements

In the state of Texas, bailiffs are not required to have special training, although there are some special training programs available. The Texas Municipal Courts Education Center offers a 12-hour training course for bailiffs and Warrant Officers. The course includes ethics, case law updates, warrant distinction and service methods, fine collection, and judicial protection. Sections on gangs and Spanish for bailiffs are also included. Bailiffs who hold a peace officer license are eligible for continuing education credits through TCLEOSE.[18]

## Role of the Bailiff

Courtroom security is an over-arching duty for bailiffs, but their job entails many things that keep the court running as well. The bailiff is the one who calls "all rise" whenever the judge enters, thus ensuring proper respect within the courtroom.[19] Bailiffs will also lead the defendant into and out of the courtroom. In some jurisdictions, bailiffs are responsible for delivering summonses requiring persons to appear in court.[20]

During a trial, the bailiff is responsible for attending to the needs of the jury both in the courtroom and during their deliberations.[21] When sequestering the jury overnight, the bailiff is responsible for ensuring they are isolated. The bailiff will contact family members and allow them to deliver clothes and other personal items, which the bailiff will then take to the juror.[22]

## Current Duties

Tom Green County:

Tom Green County received its name from General Thomas Green who served in the Civil War. The first sheriff received an appointment in 1874. Currently there are 60 deputies working for the sheriff.[23]

Tom Green County currently employs seven licensed peace officers as court bailiffs. Each bailiff works for a separate judge, including four district judges, two county court judges and one county judge. While the bailiffs work directly for a judge, their commission remains with the county sheriff.[24]

Bailiffs in Tom Green County work a full-time position. This includes attending court and other duties between sessions, generally Monday through Friday on the day shift. Starting salary is $30,000.[25]

Homeland Security has led to a tightening of security in many areas, including courthouses. Bailiffs play a major role in this enhanced security, and not just while court is in session. For example, bailiffs in Tom Green County are responsible for making arrests for anyone with an open warrant who comes into the courthouse.[26]

Tonia Jennings is a bailiff for Tom Green County Judge Mike Brown. She has been a bailiff for three years and worked other positions within the sheriff's office for six years prior to assuming this position.[27]

The county judge handles a docket consisting mostly of probate and guardianship cases. He also handles the drug court docket. The judge also attends the weekly Commissioners' Court when they are in session. The bailiff assists him in all these duties.[28]

As bailiff, Jennings is responsible for preparing court papers for misdemeanor plea bargains. This paperwork requires signatures from both the plaintiff and a representative of the County Attorney's office. The plaintiff's fingerprints must be taken and included as well.[29]

While Jennings' primary assignment is to one judge, she can rotate to other judges or courts in the county when needed. This provides her with a variety of work situations that bailiffs in other counties may not get.[30]

Among her other duties, Jennings transports sentenced individuals to the county jail where they are booked in to serve their time.[31] Booking individuals into a jail involves taking of photographs and fingerprints and completion of paperwork transferring custody from the bailiff to the jail personnel.

Organizational skill is necessary for a bailiff. Court paperwork requires proper and timely completion. The bailiff must not only keep order, but also keep things moving in order to assure the court system will continue to function.

Bexar County:

In Bexar County, bailiffs work for the sheriff's office through the Court Security and Transport Division. Members of this team transport 22,105 prisoners to court yearly. They also assist in over 100,000 cases and protect 3,500 staff members each year.[32] The Court Security and Transport Division emerged in 1985. Originally, the division had 1 clerk, 35 officers, 1 lieutenant, and 1 chief deputy. Bailiffs were directly responsible to judges from 30 different district and county courts.[33]

Most of the officers assigned to this division were 50–60 years old. Many of these men thought of the position as a form of on-the-job retirement,[34] a situation that still exists in some areas. The division has expanded through the years to respond to the increased demand for court services. Currently there are 144 persons assigned to this division. Personnel include one chief, 1 captain, 5 sergeants, 104 officers, and 35 civilian support staff members.[35]

Members of this division are responsible for providing security in the entire court complex, not just in the courtroom. To best accomplish this, some members of the division will patrol the perimeter on bicycles. The transport of prisoners to and from court in a timely fashion also enhances security by having constant activity.[36]

The increased potential for violence in the courtroom has pushed the Court Security and Transport Division to receive better training and become more professional. The old image of bailiffs as retired on the job transformed here to one of a much higher status. The division in fact contains some members of the Sheriff's Department SWAT Team to ensure they are prepared to respond rapidly and with as much force as needed to any threat.[37]

One last duty that falls to this division is to operate the Personal Recognizance Bond Satellite Booking Office. This office allows expedited paperwork and processing for persons the court permits to bond out of jail without posting monetary bail. The use of personal recognizance bonds requires the person to sign paperwork indicating their promise to return to court for their case. This type of bond is generally used with low-risk and first-time offenders, and decreases their processing time significantly.[38]

Bailiffs in Bexar County may engage in a larger variety of duties than bailiffs in other areas do, but the basic duties remain. The bailiff must provide order and security in the court complex.

## Conclusion

Bailiffs are certified law enforcement officers who work in courthouses across the state. The main responsibility of the bailiff is to make sure that the judge and the courtroom receive protection at all times.

The bailiff's job begins before court starts, with the transportation of the offender from jail. The bailiff's job continues after court has ended by returning the offender back to jail.

With the ever-increasing security needs at courthouses, whether due to actual threats or general precautions, the bailiff has remained an important player in the world of law enforcement and courts. The success of the Satellite Booking Office in Bexar County indicates the role of the bailiff does not have to be limited to just providing security. In the future, the bailiff position should expand to include more of these types of duties.

Texas Department of Parks and Wildlife, Game Warden Cynde Aguilar.

*Photo Courtesy of Cynde Aguilar.*

# Chapter 13
# Game Wardens

## Introduction

Many Criminal Justice students aspire to the position of Wildlife Law Enforcement Officer, or Game Warden. The idea of working outdoors in a natural environment, protecting animals, and working with hunters and ranchers seems very appealing. Many students, however, do not fully understand the duties that will fall on them should they attain this position.

Game wardens are involved in water safety, public education programs, Homeland Security programs, and court duties. They respond to natural disasters and provide assistance to other law enforcement agencies.[1] In fact game wardens may have the widest variety of duties of any law enforcement position discussed in this volume.

## History of the Position

From as early as 1016 there have been laws regulating wildlife and the lands where the animals live. These early laws helped to protect the wildlife, not for its own sake, but for the value the wildlife had as property of the king or landholder. Killing of a king's stag for instance could result in the death penalty.[2]

This situation remained largely unchanged until the series of revolutions that occurred across Europe in the eighteenth and nineteenth centuries. Among the other changes brought by the revolutions, was a change in hunting rights. No longer were the nobility the only ones allowed to hunt and fish. The general populace could now engage in these pursuits.[3]

Control over game in America began in Colonial days with a 1629 hunting privileges law. Several other laws concerning who could hunt, where they could hunt, and what they could hunt passed in the various colonies in this period. In fact, 12 colonies had created seasonal restrictions on hunting by 1776.[4]

The US government enacted its first game law in 1832. This law prohibited hunting game in Indian Territory. Regulation of hunting was not enough to keep game populations from becoming scarce, so efforts turned to control of predators. Ranchers and farmers were already engaging in this battle against small predators like coyotes. Government involvement in predator control focused on big game predators.[5]

Protected wildlife areas were the next step in government conservation efforts. Yellowstone National Park became the first such protected area in 1894. This effort to provide wildlife with safe places to live often combined with artificial stocking of species to promote population growth. This was especially useful for fish and bird species.[6]

When these methods proved inadequate to maintain healthy levels of wildlife, the government turned to habitat manipulation. Creating new areas for wildlife to live or improving on existing areas helps to make up for human encroachment on the natural habitat.[7]

The earliest state-level game wardens were probably in the state of Maine. These officers, often nicknamed "Moose Wardens," protected the moose populations as their primary duty.[8]

Early game wardens held political appointments. There was no official salary for these men. Pay was derived from collection of fines.[9] This system of pay surely encouraged early game wardens to be busy, and some may have even been corrupt.

Today, all 50 states have an agency responsible for enforcing fish and wildlife laws. In 2004 these 50 agencies employed 4,937 full-time sworn officers.[10] Roughly 525 of these officers are employed by Texas Department of Parks and Wildlife.[11]

## Game Wardens in Texas

Game wardens have enforced conservation laws in the state of Texas since 1895, when the Fish and Oyster Commission came into being in order to regulate fishing. The Game Department became a new part of the Fish and

Oyster Commission in 1907. The State Parks Board began in 1923. More parks and public spaces were added during the 1930s, expanding the need for state regulation.[12]

The Game, Fish and Oyster Commission changed its name in 1951 to drop the term Oyster. The newly named Game and Fish Commission merged with the State Parks Board in 1963 to become the Texas Parks and Wildlife Department.[13]

Since the beginning of state regulation over conservation laws, 16 officers have lost their lives in the line of duty. In 1919, the first two game wardens killed in the line of duty, Joe Williams and Harry Raymond, washed away in a hurricane in Aransas Bay. Since then four other officers were killed by drowning, five were murdered, four were killed in car accidents, one was killed in a small plane wreck, and one was hit by a passing car while he was on the side of the road helping a stranded motorist.[14]

The Texas Parks and Wildlife Department currently has 11 divisions. Ten of these divisions are regulatory or administrative, including Human Resources, Communications, Legal, Administrative Resources, Infrastructure, and Information Technology. Wildlife, Coastal Fisheries, Inland Fisheries, and State Parks focus on the conservation aspects of the department. Only one division, the Law Enforcement Division, contains licensed peace officers.[15]

## Modern Game Wardens

Game wardens in Texas primarily provide statewide enforcement of the Parks and Wildlife Code, but also enforce all other laws of the state. Wildlife and natural resource conservation, water safety, and related interests form the core of their responsibilities.[16]

Like other law enforcement officers in the state of Texas, game wardens may assist other agencies. Game wardens often respond to the scene of natural disasters such as Hurricanes Rita and Ike. In the words of Game Warden Aguilar, "We provided security, passed out food and water to those in the community and assisted local agencies in whatever they needed. I also did the same thing again for Hurricane Ike in 2008."[17]

Homeland Security has also given game wardens additional duties. Again, in a personal interview, Aguilar noted: "For the last few years our department has been conducting Operations on the States border and I have been involved with several operations. Anywhere from patrolling the back roads of El Paso by vehicle, to patrolling Lake Amistad by boat."[18]

## Qualifications to be a Game Warden

Potential applicants for game warden positions must pass a background check and meet these rigorous criteria:

- Never having been convicted for any Felony or Class A Misdemeanor offenses
- No conviction for any Class B Misdemeanor offense within 10 years including convictions for driving or boating while under the influence
- Never having been convicted of a domestic violence offense
- No current sentence of court-ordered community supervision, probation or parole for any criminal offense above a Class C Misdemeanor
- No current drug use
- Pass a physical conditioning test and a medical exam
- Pass a psychological exam
- No less than honorable military discharge
- No history of past peace officer license denial, revocation, nor voluntary surrender
- Must be a United States Citizen
- Must hold a Bachelors level degree from an accredited university
- Vision must be at least 20/30 with or without correction, uninterrupted peripheral vision of 140 degrees or greater, normal night vision, and ability to distinguish red and green colors
- Hearing must be at least 35 decibels or better in each ear 500, 1000, 2000 and 3000 Hz frequencies
- Possession of a valid driver's license
- Be at least 21 years of age by the date of entry into academy training. No maximum age exists[19]

Potential applicants must also agree to accept an assignment anywhere within the state of Texas. Applicants may express a preference, but assignments relate to vacancies and departmental need rather than individual preference.[20]

## Special Requirements

All persons who selected to be game wardens are required to attend the Game Warden Training Academy, currently located in Hamilton, Texas. This academy runs for approximately 30 weeks and provides in-residence training to the cadets. Cadets will receive all the training required to be certified peace officers in the state of Texas. In addition, cadets receive training in agency-specific areas such as fish, wildlife and natural resource management, water rescue, boat operations, Homeland Security, civil defense, and department administrative policies and procedures.[21]

Cadets receive a salary during their academy training. If the cadet is required to work more than 171 hours in the pay period, they may claim overtime compensation. Upon graduation, the cadet will be required to move to a duty station determined by the department. This assignment will be determined after graduation. Moving expenses are the cadet's responsibility.[22]

## Role of the Game Warden

Game wardens are responsible for promoting conservation of wildlife and natural resources through hunting and fishing regulation. Enforcement is not the only tool available to the game warden, however. A strong component of the conservation goal is the array of public education programs that the game warden will deliver. Another strong component is the set of safety programs, including boating safety and hunter safety programs.

Ultimately, game wardens represent a balance-point between nature and the human population. The ultimate goal is to promote responsible enjoyment of nature while preserving resources.

## Current Duties

The Texas Parks and Wildlife Department employs roughly 525 game wardens spread across the state. A beginning Game Warden Cadet will be paid $2,914 per month while in the six-month academy training period. After 20 years of service, a Game Warden VI will make $4,811 per month. Officers who speak a second language receive an additional $50 per month. Officers can also earn an extra $50–150 per month for educational attainment and various certifications.[23]

For game wardens, the daily routine undergoes significant seasonal modifications. "In the summer we begin patrol on lakes where we conduct Water Safety Equipment Inspections, making sure all vessels are operating in a safe manner, checking fishing license, etc. Even though it is legal to consume alcohol while operating a vessel, State law prohibits intoxicated persons (.08% BAC) from operating a boat. So throughout the day we issue citations and arrest boaters for things like Boating while Intoxicated, County and City warrants, and possession of marijuana. Other days we go kayaking down the River checking for the same violations."[24]

Hunting seasons bring game wardens out in force to check hunters, making sure poaching is not occurring. Fishing seasons are also boating seasons, which brings out water patrols at the various lakes, rivers, and coastal areas.[25]

Other seasonal activities may also occupy the time of the game warden. Hurricane season, for instance will have an effect on the daily routine, as many game wardens receive temporary assignments to relief efforts.[26]

Not everything that game wardens become involved in has a seasonal variation. Border operations are a year-round occupation. Enforcing all state laws is also a year-round occupation.[27]

Unlike many other law enforcement agencies, game wardens do not utilize the 911 system for the majority of their citizen-initiated workload. Instead, most calls from citizens come through the Operation Game Thief Hotline. This hotline is a toll-free number where citizens can report any suspected game violations.[28] The hotline operates much like a crimestopper hotline in other law enforcement contexts.[29]

## Public Education

A large portion of the duties undertaken by game wardens revolves around public education. There are at least a dozen different programs, revolving around four core areas. The areas cover outdoor learning, conservation and instructor training, resources for teachers and other leaders, and community outreach.[30]

Outdoor learning programs help introduce people to the joys of nature while at the same time teaching responsible usage. Programs falling in this area include hunter education, boater education, archery, the "Take Me Fishing" program and other programs. Outdoor learning programs exist for both rural and urban areas, making nature accessible to everyone.[31]

Community outreach programs include a Buffalo Soldiers program and a variety of grants that are available for schools and other groups. Bringing communities and organizations into the natural world is a major goal for these programs. The more people game warden programs can reach, the more support the game wardens will have from the public.[32]

The last two areas of public education are devoted to providing resources for others to be able to teach about nature or to provide the training to persons who want to become instructors in this area. Both of these areas contribute to spreading an appreciation for the natural environment. Adding instructors or persons skilled in conservation helps the game wardens spread their message of responsible use of the natural environment.[33]

## Conclusion

Game wardens work mainly with wildlife and the environment. They deal with hunters and enforce the Texas Penal Code, during all seasons. An estimated 500 wardens enforce licenses, register boats, and provide the public with local information. Additional duties consist of education programs, providing testimony in court and working with other law enforcement agencies on a needs basis.

Given the current trend toward "Green Living," game wardens will continue to be important to modern society. The large component of public education in the game warden's duties helps reinforce their importance to the community and the environment.

The game warden's intimate knowledge of the natural areas of the state makes them valuable to other law enforcement agencies as well. Enforcing border regulations will become an increasingly important duty for game wardens as they work with Homeland Security to use their knowledge of remote areas for security purposes.

Tom Green County Attorney Investigator Mickey Englert.

*Photo Courtesy of Mickey Englert.*

# Chapter 14
# District Attorney/County Attorney Investigators

## Introduction

Across the state of Texas, there are varieties of specialized investigator positions held by licensed peace officers. Many positions are so specialized that only one or two persons in the state hold them. Some special positions appear to hold authorization by statute and yet are not used anywhere. Death Investigators appear to fit this description. Texas state law authorizes their employment by coroners or medical examiners, but it appears very few if any exist.

The best example of a specialized investigator position may be within District Attorney and County Attorney Offices. This is certainly the investigative area with the most licensed peace officers.

## History and Development

Each county in the state of Texas having a County or District Attorney had to acquire authorization to create such an office from the governor. Authorization appears to have depended on the population growth and the growth in crime in each county. Once the office existed, authorization to hire additional personnel such as investigators followed the normal growth path of other government agencies. Need did not always translate into authorization, and many offices still find themselves understaffed.

Development of the investigator position appears to have happened in the 1980s regardless or how long a County or District Attorney office existed.

For example, Brazos County created its County Attorney office in the 1800s, but did not hire investigators until 1985.[1] Polk County created its District Attorney office in 1987 and employed an investigator as one of the original staff members.[2]

## District Attorney/County Attorney Investigators in Texas

District Attorneys and County Attorneys are the prosecutors for all criminal cases in their respective jurisdictions. County Attorneys may also handle civil cases. An attorney licensed by the State Bar Association occupies each position. In most cases, voters elect District Attorneys and County Attorneys to their positions. In larger departments, Assistant District Attorneys or County Attorneys may achieve positions through channels other than election.

Two-hundred-twenty-one Texas counties employ a County Attorney. The remaining 33 rely on the services of the District Attorney. County Attorneys handle cases below the level of the cases handled by the District Attorney. County Attorneys also generally perform duties as legal advisor for the county.[3]

According to Alderete, there are 202 licensed peace officers working for County Attorney offices. An additional 862 peace officers are working for District Attorney offices.[4]

## Qualifications to be District Attorney/County Attorney Investigators

Whether in a District Attorney's office or a County Attorney's office, investigators are required to be licensed peace officers. They must meet the state licensing requirements as discussed in Chapter 2.

The following requirements from the Harris County District Attorney's Office are representative of statewide requirements:

- Applicants must hold a Master Peace Officer Certification
- Residency requirements include living within 50 miles of the office
- A firearms proficiency course must be passed upon hiring[5]

Other requirements will vary depending on the office or division within the office to which a person is applying. Generally, an investigator's position is not an entry-level position attainable by a newly licensed officer.[6]

## Professional Organization

The Texas District and County Attorneys Association (TDCAA) provides a professional organization for all District and County Attorneys and their staffs in the state of Texas. This organization is non-profit and provides assistance in three core areas:

- Continuing legal education courses
- Technical assistance
- Liaison between prosecutors and other organizations[7]

Several divisions within TDCAA serve specific segments of the prosecuting community. Investigators have their own division, which provides a communication forum and investigator specific resources.[8] The open forum for investigators allows them to post questions and answers for each other, make suggestions about training needs, share relevant information, and generally keep in touch. This provides a valuable resource for investigators when dealing with strange cases, new crimes, or other issues.

## Special Requirements

There are no specific extra requirements that are state mandated for investigators in DA or County Attorney Offices. In larger offices, investigators may be required to have special skills in order to work for specific divisions. In Harris County, for example, investigators can specialize in 14 different areas, each requiring specialized skills.[9]

Many offices assigned specialized personnel to certain types of crimes such as domestic violence or cases that could result in the death penalty. Investigators in these areas may be required to have special skills or to attend specialized training.

Investigators may also attend courses provided by TDCAA. These courses include legislative updates and a course for newly hired investigators. The New DA/CA Investigator Skills Course helps those with two years or less on the job learn the basics of the job, improve their investigative skills, and develop familiarity with the court system and legal language. This course began in 2002 and occurs once a year.[10] The state does not mandate courses from TDCAA, but individual offices may make them mandatory.

## Role of the district attorney/County Attorney Investigators

Investigators for DAs' offices have their primary jurisdiction in the area covered by the DA. This may be one county in urban areas or several counties in rural areas. However, these investigators have statewide authority to enforce laws and serve criminal process.[11]

The primary duty of an investigator is to assist the District Attorney or County Attorney in achieving a conviction. The Investigator will conduct investigations, interrogations or review case files to ensure the proper collection of evidence. The Investigator's work will often end up before a Grand Jury and will help determine if an Indictment will be forthcoming.[12]

Investigators have to think about their work differently from regular peace officers. Regular officers are often under pressure to move rapidly from case to case. Closing a case is a priority. An investigator in a DA or County Attorney office has to be concerned with the types of evidence that were or were not collected and other details of the case. Convincing a jury the defendant is guilty is the priority.[13]

## Current Duties

An informal survey of counties surrounding Johnson County revealed a salary range for investigators ranging from $30,000 to $50,000. Many counties offered incentive pay for investigators who achieved intermediate, advanced, or master peace officer status. Additionally, some counties permit the investigator to take their car home, and offer additional benefits to be competitive.[14]

Polk County District Attorney Investigators:

The DA's office in Polk County emerged in 1987. Then-Governor William P. "Bill" Clements appointed Don F. Keith as the first DA. The new DA's office had only Keith, a secretary, and an investigator. The team succeeded in having 49 indictments returned that first year.[15]

By 2007, the Polk County DA's office had expanded to 13 employees. The case numbers had also risen to 819 indictments, 170 no-billed or dismissed cases, and 29 cases that were re-filed. These cases covered both misdemeanors and felonies.[16]

The Polk County DA's office employs six Assistant DAs and four sworn peace officers who act as investigators. These investigators earn around $36,740 per year. They can add an additional $75 per month for achieving advanced levels of peace officer certification.[17]

W. D. "Bill" Willis was a Senior Felony District Attorney Investigator with the Polk County DA's office for six years. His background includes seven years with military police, five years as an adult probation officer, one year as a deputy constable, and three years with corporate security.[18]

The list of duties handled by Willis is long and demonstrates the variety of experiences available within this position.

- Enforce all criminal laws of the state
- Liaise with local law enforcement agencies to assist them in filing cases for prosecution
- Expedited filing of cases
- Quality control of criminal case intake for felony filings
- Liaise with law enforcement agencies within state and inter-state areas to provide assistance in apprehension of fugitives, prosecution, and sentencing of criminals
- Receive complaints of criminal activity
- Conduct investigations and file supporting criminal process service culminating in arrest or inputting electronic warrant information
- Booking arrested suspects when necessary
- Testifying in local and other courts of competent jurisdiction[19]

Like many law enforcement jobs, DA Investigators spend much of their time on paperwork. According to Willis, 85 percent of his job involved paperwork such as filing cases with the Grand Jury. Only 15 percent of his time involved tracking suspects, making arrests, or otherwise enforcing laws.[20]

Much of Willis's job involved some form of research. Sometimes this meant legal research prior to filing a case. Other times this meant locating a witness to serve with a subpoena. Locating records for subpoena also often involved research.[21]

Cases assigned to an investigator tend to be the most serious or complicated. These can also be the most difficult for the investigator. Willis[22] indicates that "Child deaths and child sexual assaults were the most difficult to maintain professional distance."

According to Willis, it is not just 9-11 that has changed law enforcement. Television has also had an effect. Willis often spent time with the Grand Jury and trial juries. Even when he personally was not in front of the jury, his work would be. Television shows like *CSI* have changed the way a jury looks at a case. More questions arise about why police did not conduct such-and-such type of forensic test.[23]

### County Attorney Investigators:

The County Attorney's Office in Tom Green County houses the County Attorney and four Assistant County Attorneys. One of these assistants works primarily in the Domestic Violence Division. In addition to the County Attorneys, the office employs two investigators, one of whom is assigned to the Domestic Violence Division and the other to the other cases.[24]

Chief Investigator Mickey Englert has been with the Tom Green County Attorney's Office since 2001. Englert has been a licensed peace officer since 1972. He retired from the San Angelo Police Department in 1987.[25]

The chief investigator position came about in 1992. The investigator's commission operates through the sheriff's office. Base salary for investigators ranges from $24,000–32,000.[26]

Since 9-11, the agency has received a minimal amount of equipment or grant money from Homeland Security. Anything received from Homeland Security comes through the sheriff's office.[27]

Investigators in County Attorney offices have a variety of responsibilities. One responsibility is to assist the County Attorney in preparing for trial if one is necessary. An estimated 90 percent of offenders plead out, resulting in no need for a trial. Another responsibility is working returned check cases. Anything over $1500 processes through District Court as a felony.[28]

"For an investigator, there is no typical day. You visit with victims as well as offenders. You find yourself becoming a liaison between the victim and County Attorney office."[29]

## Other Offices:

In Harris County, the County Attorney office employs 90 attorneys and 130 support staff. In addition to prosecutorial work, the County Attorney is responsible for providing legal representation to county employees while engaged in county business. Representation extends to the hospital district, the flood control district, Child Protective Services, the Harris County Guardianship Program (Adult Protective Services), and some state offices.[30] Much of this work relates to civil cases and investigators may or may not play a role depending on the particular case.

In Brazos County, the County Attorney office employs 12 attorneys and 5 full-time investigators. One part-time investigator and several support staff also work in this office. In this office, investigators may work on their own cases and each year the investigators serve hundreds of warrants for theft. Warrant service is secondary to preparing a case for court so this activity occurs when time permits.[31]

According to Investigator Sergeant Scott Biddle[32] with the Brazos County Attorney Office, technology has affected the filing of cases. More witnesses and more physical evidence exist in each case due to the impact of computers and other technology. Cases are thus more complicated and time consuming. Additionally, this will have an impact on the need for well-trained investigators with technological skills.

## Beyond Paperwork:

Paperwork is far from the only activity investigators will engage in. Investigators are peace officers for a reason. Warrant service can entail seeking out persons who may pose a threat to the investigator. Investigators may also have to pursue suspects and make arrests, sometimes in less than ideal conditions. Biddle once chased a naked suspect into an attic space.

"Even with a good flashlight I could not see very far through and between the rafters. I continued to announce my presence and authority but got no reply. After searching for several minutes I saw a face sticking up out of the blown fiberglass insulation. The suspect had laid down between two rafters and pulled insulation over his entire body concealing everything but his face. I began giving him verbal commands and approached him. As I turned him over to cuff him and the insulation began to fall away I saw he was completely naked. I was completely soaked with sweat as an attic in Texas in the summer can easily be 120–140 degrees. The suspect was just as covered in sweat and insulation was sticking to everything. I got him up and walked him back towards the access panel where another officer was waiting. As we got to the access panel the other officer began to reach up for the suspect to bring him down through the hole and I warned him that the suspect was naked, sweaty, and covered in insulation. The officer went in the bedroom and found a pair of sweatpants and held them up with the waist opened. I picked up the suspect with a hand below each armpit and lowered him down through the hole and the other officer slid the sweatpants onto him as I lowered him down. We never could get an answer from him why he was naked."[33]

While the investigators engage in a variety of research and fieldwork, they do not answer 911 calls, and are therefore more able to schedule their own time. The job requires self-motivation and an ability to work independently to complete cases. Utilization of the investigators depends on the policies in each office.[34]

## Conclusion

The investigators with District Attorney or County Attorney offices play an important role in ensuring our justice system does not fail us. Their work is instrumental in ensuring successful prosecutions.

There may also be other isolated specialized investigator positions available across the state of Texas, like Death Investigators. Each one plays a special role in the law enforcement world; however, an exhaustive review of these positions would be impossible and would add little to the description already provided in this chapter. At the core, any investigator engages in similar tasks; it is just the subject matter that differs.

# Chapter 15
# Conclusion

If readers have learned nothing else from this book, they should now know a lot more about the massive variety of law enforcement positions available in the state of Texas. Texas may in fact have more variety in law enforcement than any other state. Positions like investigators with the Texas Racing Commission demonstrate this variety. Only six such agencies exist in the United States and Texas has one.

Within all this variety of law enforcement, there still exists a multitude of similarities between these positions. Just being a peace officer in the state of Texas requires standard training. All Texas peace officers thus have a similar training background.

The similarities continue from the basic training level. Officers must continually achieve training to keep updated in the field. Some subjects, like Multiculturalism, are required of all officers. Additionally, many of the positions have specific authorization to perform the same duties. Constables, for example, may conduct routine traffic stops in the same way as city police officers.

Many of the specialized jobs in Texas law enforcement require prior law enforcement experience. The investigator with many District Attorney's Offices must have prior law enforcement experience in order to possess a Master Peace Officer Certification and thus to be qualified for the position.

While not normally a specific job requirement, most law enforcement officers will need to cooperate with other law enforcement agencies at some point in their career. Many agencies will join together for responses to specific situations. Hurricane relief is one such situation. Officers from TABC, the Texas Parks and Wildlife Department, and other agencies all responded to the Gulf Coast to help relief and recovery efforts.

Homeland Security creates another area where agencies can work together. An increasing amount of money, training, and resources is available for agencies to enhance security, be more prepared for emergencies, or conduct operations along the border.

All of these similarities should be comforting to persons looking for jobs within law enforcement. Similarities mean each officer has a common background and set of experiences. Working with other agencies is not prohibitive, nor should seeking a specialized law enforcement position.

The similarities may make job applicants more comfortable, but the differences in positions are a good thing. In the world of Texas law enforcement, there is something for everyone. Applicants need only look around.

Differences in law enforcement positions range from small to huge, depending on the position. Each position carries with it a unique set of challenges. Elected officers face pressure from the voters whereas non-elected officers seem free from this pressure. Over-enforcement, under-enforcement, use of force, and use of deadly force can create controversy for any officer or department. Budget shortfalls also create controversy over staffing and activity levels.

Today's law enforcement positions are becoming very competitive. Since Homeland Security is expanding positions, the focus now is on how much patrol experience the officer possesses. For example, in the past, law enforcement mainly hired officers who had jailer experience. The thought was if you could work the jail, you could handle anything. After all, the patrol officer would drop the offender off at the jail and leave. It was the jailer's problem now to process and hold the offender. That trend is changing. The more street patrol experience the peace officer has, the more qualified they are for specialized policing agencies.

Technology is also changing the law enforcement world. Officers with computer or other technological experience are preferred over those who lack this expertise. Identity theft and computer crimes are increasing this need; however, many departments find it difficult to hire persons with the technological experience to investigate these crimes.

Overall, Texas has a huge variety of law enforcement agencies and a wide variety of positions within these agencies. The need for qualified personnel will, in all likelihood, expand in the future. Persons possessing the proper skills and training will be in high demand and can choose their area according to their own needs and desires.

# Endnotes

## Chapter 1

1. Walker, S. (1983). *The police in America: An introduction.* New York: McGraw Hill. p. 35.

2. Ibid., p. 36.

3. Babbie, E. R. (2006). *The practice of social research.* (11th ed.). Belmont, CA: Wadsworth.

4. Anderson, D. C. (1995). *Crime and the politics of hysteria: How the Willie Horton story changed American justice.* New York: Times Books, Random House.

5. Associated Press. (2010, December 20) Angry crowd seeks answers after groom's wedding day shooting. Fox News. Retrieved from http://www.foxnews.com/story/0,2933,231968,00.html.

6. Williams, J. (2006, February 20) Personal Communication. Former Director of Enforcement, Texas Racing Commission.

7. U.S. Census Bureau. State and County Quick Facts. Texas. (n.d.) Retrieved December 20, 2010 from http://quickfacts.census.gov/qfd/states/48000.html

8. Pelz, B., & Pelz, T. (2001). *Introduction to criminal justice: Texas edition.* Belmont, CA: Wadsworth.

9. Ibid.

10. Mange, Tela. (2006, November 29) Personal Communication. Texas Department of Public Safety.

11. Holbrooks, J. W. (2008, January 10) Personal Communication. Constable, Precinct 2, Crosby County, TX.

12. Horton, D. M., & Turner, R. K. (1999). *Lone star justice: A comprehensive overview of the Texas criminal justice system.* Austin, TX: Eakin Press.

13. Pelz & Pelz (2001). *Introduction to criminal justice.*

14. Horton & Turner (1999). *Lone star justice.*

15. Butler-Kay, K., & Graham, J. (2000). *Criminal justice in Texas.* Boston: Allyn and Bacon.

16. Ibid.

17. The Texas Uniform Crime Reporting Program (n.d.) Retrieved December 20, 2010, from http://www.txdps.state.tx.us/administration/crime_records/pages/ucr.htm

18. Ibid.

19. 2009 Crime in Texas (n.d.) Retrieved December 20, 2010 from http://www.txdps.state.tx.us/crimereports/09/09UCR27.pdf#page=66

20. Gaines, L. H., & Miller, R. L. (2009). *Criminal justice in action.* (5th ed). Belmont, CA: Thompson Wadsworth.

21. Ibid.

22. Ibid.

23. Texas Department of Public Safety (n.d.) Retrieved December 20, 2010 from http://www.txdps.state.tx.us

24. Gaines & Miller (2009). *Criminal justice in action*.

25. Ibid.

26. Ibid.

27. Alderete, Lillian. (2006, September 22) Personal Communication. Texas Commission on Law Enforcement Officer Standards and Education.

28. Mange, Tela. (2006, November 29) Personal Communication. Texas Department of Public Safety.

29. Alderete, Lillian. (2006, September 22) Personal Communication. Texas Commission on Law Enforcement Officer Standards and Education.

## Chapter 2

1. History and jail concepts. (n.d.) Retrieved December 20, 2010, from www.tcleose.state.tx.us/Documents/training/1007_1_hist_jail_concept.doc

2. Ibid.

3. Field Support Services. (n.d.) Retrieved December 20, 2010, from www.tcleose.state.tx.us/content/field_support.cfm

4. Procedure for Qualifying Applicants for Employment as Peace Officers. (2004, September 1). Retrieved December 20, 2010, from http://www.utsystem.edu/pol/jobs.html

5. Law Enforcement Academy. (n.d.) Retrieved December 20, 2010 from http://www.sulross.edu/pages/3204.asp

6. Macias, Michael. (2010, November 29) Personal Communication. Law Enforcement Academy, Sul Ross State University.

7. Recruiting Office. (2010, September 7) Personal Communication. Dallas Police Department

8. How to become a Texas peace officer. (n.d.) Retrieved December 20, 2010, from http://www.classen-buck.com/id113.htm

9. Ibid.

10. Dempsey, J. S., & Forst, L. S. (2005). *An introduction to policing.* (3rd ed.). Belmont, CA: Wadsworth.

11. L-1 Report of Appointment/License Application. (n.d.) Retrieved December 20, 2010, from http://www.TCLEOSE.state.tx.us

12. How to become a Texas peace officer. (n.d.) Retrieved December 20, 2010, from http://www.classen-buck.com/id113.htm

13. Dempsey & Forst (2005). *An introduction to policing.*

14. How to become a Texas peace officer. (n.d.) Retrieved December 20, 2010, from http://www.classen-buck.com/id113.htm

15. Dempsey & Forst (2005). *An introduction to policing.*

16. How to become a Texas peace officer. (n.d.) Retrieved December 20, 2010, from http://www.classen-buck.com/id113.htm

17. Ibid.

18. Dempsey & Forst (2005). *An introduction to policing.*

19. How to become a Texas peace officer. (n.d.) Retrieved December 20, 2010, from http://www.classen-buck.com/id113.htm

20. Dempsey & Forst (2005). *An introduction to policing.*

21. How to become a Texas peace officer. (n.d.) Retrieved December 20, 2010, from http://www.classen-buck.com/id113.htm

22. Walker, S. (1983). *The police in America: An introduction.* New York: McGraw Hill.

23. Dempsey & Forst (2005). *An introduction to policing.*

24. Warning. (n.d.). Retrieved December 20, 2010 from www.tcleose.state.tx.us/training-warning-05.asp

25. Certification Requirements Chart. (2006, April 12). Retrieved December 20, 2010, from http://www.tcleose.state.tx.us/FormsApps/2006/04_06/Cert_Chart.doc

26. Ibid.

27. Ibid.

28. Ibid.

## Chapter 3

1. Kanovitz J., & Kanovitz M. (2005). *Constitutional Law* (10th ed.) New York: Matthew Bender and Co., chap. 1.

2. US Constitution, Amendment 10. Electronic Copy. Retrieved April 12, 2010, from http://caselaw.lp.findlaw.com/data/constitution/amendments.html.

3. Kanovitz & Kanovitz, op.cit., pp. 9–19.

4. LaFave W. R. (2003). *Criminal Law* (4th ed.) St. Paul: Thomson-West, pp. 193-197.

5. Kanovitz & Kanovitz, op. cit., pp. 9–19.

6. Rotunda, R., & Nowak, J. (1999). *Treatise on Constitutional Law*, vol. 1. St. Paul: West Group, p. 217.

7. E.g., Kanovitz & Kanovitz, op. cit.

8. Horton, D. M., & Turner, R. K. (1999). *Lone star justice: A comprehensive overview of the Texas criminal justice system.* Austin, TX: Eakin Press, p. 87.

9. Texas Constitution, Article 5 sec .18 and 23. Electronic Copy. Retrieved 2010, April 12, from http://bb2.tlc.state.tx.us/txconst/sections/cn000500-001800.html

10. Texas Jurisprudence 3rd. (2007). Vol. 59, "Police Constables and Sheriffs," San Francisco: Bancroft Whitney, sec. 34.

11. Ibid., sec. 1-55.

12. Texas Government Code. Electronic Copy. Retrieved, 2010, April 12. from http://tlo2.tlc.state.tx.us/statutes/gov.toc.htm. All references to this Code are from this source.

13. E.g., Texas Education Code, sec. 51.212 and 51.214. Electronic Copy. Retrieved 2006, Aug. 1, from http://tlo2.tlc.state.tx.us/statutes/ed.toc.htm. All references to the Education Code are from this source.

14. Texas Local Government Code. Electronic Copy. Retrieved 2007, Jan. 1 from http://tlo2.tlc.state.tx.us/statutes/lg.toc.htm. All references to the Local Government Code are from this source.

15. Texas Penal Code. Retrieved 2010, April 12 from http://tlo2.tlc.state.tx.us/statutes/pe.toc.htm. All references to the Penal Code are from this source.

16. Texas Code of Criminal Procedure. Electronic Copy. Retrieved 2010, April. 12, from http://tlo2.tlc.state.tx.us/statutes/cr.toc.htm. All references to the Code of Criminal Procedure are from this source.

17. Reamey, G. S., & Harkins, D. J. (1988). "Warrantless arrest jurisdiction in Texas: An analysis and proposal," *Saint Mary's Law Journal*, 19, fn. 106, 107 and 108.

18. Texas Jurisprudence, op. cit., sec. 1.

19. Reamey & Harkins, op. cit., pp. 858.

20. Texas Jurisprudence, op. cit., sec. 1. 3rd, "Police, Constable and Sheriffs," sec. 1. (g); Reamey & Harkins, op. cit.

21. Texas Jurisprudence, op. cit., sec. 57; Texas Code of Criminal Procedure, Article 14.03 (d).

22. Reamey & Harkins, op. cit. pp. 858–859.

23. Nichols, L. D., Robbins, R. K., & Harrelson, D. B. (2004). *The Texas Peace Officer* (9th ed.) vol. 1, Richmond CA: McCutcheon, chap. 1.

24. Ibid., p. 26.

25. Ibid., p. 55.

26. Ibid.

27. Ibid., p. 56.

28. Texas Family Code. Electronic Copy. Retrieved 2010, April 12, from http://tlo2.tlc.statetx.us/statutes/fa. toc.htm. All references to the Family Code are from this source.

29. Nichols, L. D., Robbins, R. K., & Harrelson, D. B. (2004). *The Texas Peace Officer* (9th ed.) vol. 2. Richmond CA: McCutcheon, chap. 24.

30. Nichols, Robbins & Harrelson, vol. 1, op. cit., chap. 9; Texas Alcoholic Beverage Code. Electronic Copy. Retrieved 2010, April. 12, from http://tlo2.tlc.state.tx.us/statutes/al.toc.htm. All references to the Alcoholic Beverage Code are from this source.

31. Nichols, Robbins & Harrelson, vol. 1, op. cit., chap. 7.

32. Nichols, Robbins & Harrelson, vol. 1, op. cit., pp. 360-388; Texas Transportation Code. Electronic Copy. Retrieved 2010, April 12, from http://tlo2.tlc.state.tx.us/statutes/tn.toc.htm. All references to the Transportation Code are from this source.

33. Nichols, Robbins & Harrison, vol. 1, op. cit, chap. 11.

34. Nicholson, Robbins & Harrelson, vol. 2, op.cit., chap. 10; Texas Health and Safety Code. Electronic Copy. Retrieved 2010, April. 12, from http://tlo2.tlc.state.tx.us/statutes/hs.oc.htm. All references to the Health and Safety Code are from this source.

35. *Miranda v. Arizona*, 384 U.S. 436, 1966.

36. Meeker J. (2005). Arrest, Search and Seizure without a warrant manual, Pflugerville, TX: CLEAR; Meeker, J. (2003). Search Warrant Manual, Pflugerville, TX: CLEAR; LexisNexis (2007). Texas Criminal Law and Traffic Law Manual, Charlottesville, VA: LexisNexis, pp. LG-47–48.

37. Meeker, Search Warrant Manual, op. cit., chap. 4.

38. del Carmen, R. V. (2007). *Criminal Procedure*. Belmont, CA: Thomson-Wadsworth, p. 63; See Texas Code of Criminal Procedure, Article 18.20.

# Endnotes

39. Meeker, Without a Warrant, op. cit., p. 45; *Davis v. State*, 992 S.W.2d 218 (Tex.Crim. App. 1992).

40. Holtz, L. E., & Spencer, W. J. (2004). *Texas contemporary criminal procedure.* Longwood, FL: Gould, p. 29.

41. *Michigan Dept. of State Police v. Sitz*, 496 U.S. 444 (1990)

42. *Holt v. State*, 887 S.W.2d. 16 (TexCrim.App. 1994)

43. Meeker, Without a Warrant, op. cit. p. 63; Lexis-Nexis (2008). Texas Criminal Law and Traffic Manual, 2007-2008 ed. Charlottesville, VA: LexisNexis, p. LG-10.

44. *McMillan v. State*, 609 S.W.2d. 784 (Tex.Crim.App. 1980).

45. LexisNexis, op. cit., pp. ix-xvi, LH1-LH6; S. Edmonds. (2005). 2005–2007 Legislative Update. Austin: Texas District and County Attorneys Association.

46. One important area that has received only cursory attention herein is the service and execution of process in civil and criminal cases. Because of their complexity, liability issues have been omitted. See Nichols, L. D., Robbins, R. K., & Harrelson, D. B. (2006). *The Texas Peace Officer* (10th ed.) Richmond CA: McCutcheon, chap. 11.

## Chapter 4

1. Walker, S. (1983). *The police in America: An introduction.* New York: McGraw Hill.

2. Haskins, C. H. (1960). *Norman institutions.* New York: Frederick Ungar Publishing Co.

3. Baker, T. (1966). *The Normans.* New York: The MacMillan Company.

4. Haskins (1960). *Norman institutions.*

5. Baker (1966). *The Normans.*

6. Roth, M. P. (2005). *Crime and punishment: A history of the criminal justice system.* Belmont, CA: Wadsworth.

7. A brief history of constables in the English speaking world. (n.d.). Retrieved 2010, December 20, from http://www.russianbooks.org/crime/cph1.htm

8. The early history of constables. (n.d.). Retrieved 2010, December 20, from http://dentoncounty.com/dept/cn1/history.htm

9. History on Constables. (2000). Retrieved 2010, December 20, from http://www.constable.com/history.html

10. Hatley, A. G. (1999). *Texas constables: A frontier heritage.* Lubbock: Texas Tech University Press.

11. A brief history of constables in the English speaking world. (n.d.). Retrieved 2010, December 20, from http://www.russianbooks.org/crime/cph1.htm

12. Ibid.

13. Ibid.

14. Hatley (1999). *Texas constables.*

15. A brief history of constables in the English speaking world. (n.d.). Retrieved 2010, December 20, from http://www.russianbooks.org/crime/cph1.htm

16. History of the constable in colonial America. (n.d.). Retrieved 2010, December 20, from http://www.wilco.org/CountyDepartments/Constables/HistoryoftheConstable/tabid/564/language/en-US/Default.aspx

17. The early history of constables. (n.d.). Retrieved 2010, December 20, from http://dentoncounty.com/dept/cn1/history.htm

18. Richardson, J. F. (1975). The early years of the New York Police Department. In J. Skolnick & T. Gray (Eds), *Police in America*. Boston: Little, Brown.

19. Hatley (1999). *Texas constables*.

20. Ibid.

21. Early history of the constable. (n.d.). Retrieved 2010, December 20, from http://www.wilco.org/CountyDepartments/Constables/HistoryoftheConstable/tabid/564/language/en-US/Default.aspx

22. Hatley, A. G. (1999). *Texas constables: A frontier heritage*. Lubbock: Texas Tech University Press.

23. The early history of constables. (n.d.). Retrieved 2010, December 20, from http://dentoncounty.com/dept/cn1/history.htm

24. Butler-Kay, K., & Graham, J. (2000). *Criminal justice in Texas*. Boston: Allyn and Bacon.

25. What is a constable? (n.d.). Retrieved 2010, December 20, from http://www.bexar.org/constable/pct4/History/history.html

26. Hatley (1999). *Texas constables*.

27. What is a constable? (n.d.). Retrieved 2010, December 20, from http://www.bexar.org/constable/pct4/History/history.html

28. Horton, D. M., & Turner, R. K. (1999). *Lone star justice: A comprehensive overview of the Texas criminal justice system*. Austin, TX: Eakin Press.

29. Constable (n.d.) Retrieved 2010, December 20, from http://www.tshaonline.org/handbook/online/articles/CC/mbc5.html

30. History of the Texas Constable. (n.d.). Retrieved 2010, December 20, from http://www.williamson-county.org/CountyDepartments/Constables/HistoryoftheConstable/tabid/564/language/en-US/Default.aspx

31. The early history of constables. (n.d.). Retrieved 2010, December 20, from http://dentoncounty.com/dept/cn1/history.htm

32. Early history of the constable. (n.d.). Retrieved 2010, December 20, from http://www.wilco.org/CountyDepartments/Constables/HistoryoftheConstable/tabid/564/language/en-US/Default.aspx

33. John Wesley Hardin. (n.d.). Retrieved 2010, December 20, from http://www.tshaonline.org/handbook/online/articles/HH/fha63.html

34. Alderete, Lillian. (2006, September 22) Personal Communication. Texas Commission on Law Enforcement Officer Standards and Education.

35. History of the Texas Constable. (n.d.). Retrieved 2010, December 20, from http://www.williamson-county.org/CountyDepartments/Constables/HistoryoftheConstable/tabid/564/language/en-US/Default.aspx

36. What is a constable? (n.d.). Retrieved 2010, December 20, from http://www.bexar.org/constable/pct4/History/history.html

37. Pelz, B., & Pelz, T. (2001). *Introduction to criminal justice: Texas edition*. Belmont, CA: Wadsworth.

38. What are constables? (n.d.). Retrieved 2010, December 20, from http://www.tomselman.com

# Endnotes

39. Ibid.

40. Constable training requirements. (n.d.). Retrieved 2010, December 20, from http://www.tcleose.state.tx.us/content/licensing_certifications.cfm

41. Texas Constitution, Article 5 sec. 18 subsection h. Retrieved 2010, December 20, from http://www.statutes.legis.state.tx.us/Docs/CN/htm/CN.5.htm

42. Ibid.

43. Texas Constitution, Article 5. Retrieved 2010, December 20, from http://www.statutes.legis.state.tx.us/Docs/CN/htm/CN.5.htm

44. Constable training requirements. (n.d.). Retrieved 2010, December 20, from http://www.tcleose.state.tx.us/content/licensing_certifications.cfm

45. What is a constable? (n.d.). Retrieved 2010, December 20, from http://www.bexar.org/constable/pct4/History/history.html

46. History on Constables. (2000). Retrieved 2010, December 20, from http://www.constable.com/history.html

47. Powers and duties. (n.d.). Retrieved 2010, December 20, from http://www.elliscountyconstable.org/373.html

48. What is a constable? (n.d.). Retrieved 2010, December 20, from http://www.bexar.org/constable/pct4/History/history.html

49. Tarrant County Constables. (n.d.). Retrieved 2010, December 20, from http://www.tarrantcounty.com/eConstable/site/default.asp

50. Horton & Turner (1999). *Lone star justice*.

51. Hester, Alvie (2007, October 20) Personal Communication. Constable, Precinct 4, Tom Green County.

52. Texas Constitution, Article 5. Retrieved 2010, December 20, from http://www.statutes.legis.state.tx.us/Docs/CN/htm/CN.5.htm

53. Ibid.

54. Ibid.

55. Holbrooks, J. W. (2008, January 10) Personal Communication. Constable, Precinct 2, Crosby County, TX.

56. Ibid.

57. Ibid.

58. Ibid.

59. Ibid.

60. Ibid.

61. Ibid.

62. Ibid.

63. Ibid.

64. Welcome to Wichita County, Texas. (n.d.) Retrieved 2010, December 20, from http://www.co.Wichita.tx.us/

65. Brewer, Mark (2008, January 7) Personal Communication. Constable, Precinct 1, Wichita County, Texas.

66. Ibid.

67. Brewer, Mark (2007, December 17) Personal Communication. Constable, Precinct 1, Wichita County, Texas.

68. Adamcik, Ben (2007, October 26) Personal Communication. Constable, Precinct 3, Dallas County, Texas.

69. Ibid.

70. Timms, E., & Krause, K. (2009, October 25). Dallas County constable's growing ticketing said to boost safety and county coffers. *The Dallas Morning News*, Retrieved 2010, December 20, from http://www.dallasnews.com/sharedcontent/dws/news/localnews/stories/DN-constabletraffic_25met.ART.State.Edition2.4bdbc5f.html

71. Ibid.

72. Jaurez, Augustine (2007, October 30) Personal Communication. Constable, Precinct 4, Webb County, Texas.

73. Martinez, Sonia (2007, December 17) Personal Communication. Payroll Clerk, Webb County, Texas.

74. Hester, Alvie (2007, October 20) Personal Communication. Constable, Precinct 4, Tom Green County.

75. Ibid.

76. Ibid.

77. Koca, Jim (2006, January 2) Personal Communication. Criminal Justice Director, Concho Valley Council of Governments.

78. Cobb, Joan (2007, August 12) Personal Communication. Deputy Constable, Precinct 4, Tom Green County.

79. Koca, Jim (2006, January 2) Personal Communication. Criminal Justice Director, Concho Valley Council of Governments.

80. Cobb, Joan (2007, August 12) Personal Communication. Deputy Constable, Precinct 4, Tom Green County.

81. Ibid.

82. Ibid.

83. Ibid.

84. Senate Resolution 250. Retrieved 2010, December 20, from http://www.journals.senate.state.tx.us/sjrnl/79r/html/sj03-01-f.htm

85. Bill Blackwood Law Enforcement Management Institute of Texas (n.d.) Retrieved 2010, December 20, from http://www.lemitonline.org/

## Chapter 5

1. Williams, J. H. (1988). *A great and shining road: The epic story of the transcontinental railroad*. New York: Times Books.

2. Amtrak National Facts (2008). Retrieved 2010, December 20, from http://www.amtrak.com/servlet/ContentServer?pagename=Amtrak/am2Copy/Title _Image_Copy_Page&c=am2 Copy&cid=1081442674300&ssid=542

3. Amtrak Fact Sheet, Fiscal Year 2008: State of Texas (2008). Retrieved 2010, December 20, from http://www.amtrak.com/pdf/factsheets/TEXAS08.pdf

4. Homeland Security (n.d.) Retrieved 2010, December 20, from http://www.bnsf.com/tools/resourceprotection/homeland_security.html

# Endnotes

5. Stover, J. F. (1961) American railroads. Chicago: University of Chicago Press.

6. The First Known Train Robbery in the U.S. (n.d.) Retrieved 2010, December 20, from: http://www.americaslibrary.gov/cgi-bin/page.cgi/jb/recon/robbery

7. Stover, J. F. (1961). *American railroads*. Chicago: University of Chicago Press.

8. Dewhurst, H. S. (1955). *The railroad police*. Springfield, IL: Thomas Books.

9. Ibid.

10. Ibid.

11. Mares, L. (2009, February 10) Personal Communication. Special Agent in Charge, BNSF Railway Police.

12. The Mid Twentieth Century (n.d.) Retrieved 2010, December 20, from http://www.therailroadpolice.com/history.htm

13. Ibid.

14. Ibid.

15. Reaves, B. A. (2007). *Census of State and Local Law Enforcement Agencies, 2004.* Washington D.C.: Bureau of Justice Statistics.

16. Block, L. (2009, February 24). Personal Communication. Texas Department of Public Safety.

17. Where the Road Meets the Rail (n.d.) Retrieved 2010, December 20, from http://tti.tamu.edu/publications/researcher/newsletter.htm?vol=35&issue=2&article=1

18. Texas and Pacific Railroad Police Department Fort Worth, TX (n.d.) Retrieved 2010, December 20, from http://www.odmp.org/agency/4464-texas-and-pacific-railroad-police-department-railroad-police

19. Dallas Terminal and Railway Company Police Department Dallas, TX (n.d.) Retrieved 2010, December 20, from http://www.odmp.org/agency/5506-dallas-terminal-and-railway-company-police-department-railroad-police

20. Fort Worth and Denver Railroad Police Department Wichita Falls, TX (n.d.) Retrieved 2010, December 20, from http://www.odmp.org/agency/5196-fort-worth-and-denver-railroad-police-department-railroad-police

21. Matthews, C. (2009, January 5) Personal Communication. Chief Special Agent. BNSF Railway Police.

22. Ibid.

23. Ibid.

24. Green, D. (2009, February 20) Personal Communication. Senior Special Agent. Union Pacific Railroad Police.

25. Mares, L. (2009, February 10) Personal Communication. Special Agent in Charge, BNSF Railway Police.

26. Railroad Special Agent (n.d.) Retrieved 2010, December 20, from http://www.bnsf.com/tools/resourceprotection/railroad_special_agent.html

27. Early Days of Railroad Policing to Present (n.d.) Retrieved 2010, December 20, from http://www.therailroadpolice.com/history.htm#Early%20Days%20of%20Railroad%20Policing%20to%20present

28. Railroad Police Officers, Title 49 USC sec 207.2 Retrieved 2010, December 20, From http://law.justia.com/us/cfr/title49/49-4.1.1.1.3.html

29. Block, L. (2009, February 24) Personal Communication. Public Information Officer, Texas Department of Public Safety.

30. Railroad Police Officers, Title 49 USC sec 207.2 Retrieved 2010, December 20, From http://law.justia.com/us/cfr/title49/49-4.1.1.1.3.html

31. Ibid.

32. Public Law 106-110 (Nov 24, 1999) 106th Congress.

33. Early Days of Railroad Policing to Present (n.d.) Retrieved 2010, December 20, from http://www.therailroadpolice.com/history.htm#Early%20Days%20of%20Railroad%20Policing%20to%20present

34. Mares, L. (2009, February 10) Personal Communication. Special Agent in Charge, BNSF Railway Police.

35. Green, D. (2009, February 20) Personal Communication. Senior Special Agent. Union Pacific Railroad Police.

36. Matthews, C. (2009, January 5) Personal Communication. Chief Special Agent. BNSF Railway Police.

37. Ibid.

38. Ibid.

39. Railroad Special Agent (n.d.) Retrieved 2010, December 20, from http://www.bnsf.com/tools/resourceprotection/railroad_special_agent.html

40. Canine Police (n.d.) Retrieved 2010, December 20, from http://www.bnsf.com/tools/resourceprotection/canine.html

41. Mares, L. (2009, February 10) Personal Communication. Special Agent in Charge, BNSF Railway Police.

42. Green, D. (2009, February 20) Personal Communication. Senior Special Agent. Union Pacific Railroad Police.

43. Matthews, C. (2009, January 5) Personal Communication. Chief Special Agent. BNSF Railway Police.

44. Mares, L. (2009, February 10) Personal Communication. Special Agent in Charge, BNSF Railway Police.

45. Ibid.

46. Matthews, C. (2009, January 5) Personal Communication. Chief Special Agent. BNSF Railway Police.

47. Ibid.

48. Mares, L. (2009, February 10) Personal Communication. Special Agent in Charge, BNSF Railway Police.

49. Matthews, C. (2009, January 5) Personal Communication. Chief Special Agent. BNSF Railway Police.

50. Police Solutions (n.d.) Retrieved 2010, December 20, from http://www.bnsf.com/tools/resourceprotection/police_services.html

51. Matthews, C. (2009, January 5) Personal Communication. Chief Special Agent. BNSF Railway Police.

52. Ibid.

53. Ibid.

Endnotes 159

54. Mares, L. (2009, February 10) Personal Communication. Special Agent in Charge, BNSF Railway Police.

55. Ibid.

56. Ibid.

57. Green, D. (2009, February 20) Personal Communication. Senior Special Agent. Union Pacific Railroad Police.

58. Ibid.

59. Ibid.

60. Matthews, C. (2009, January 5) Personal Communication. Chief Special Agent. BNSF Railway Police.

61. Citizens for Rail Safety (n.d.) Retrieved 2010, December 20, from http://www.bnsf.com/tools/resourceprotection/crs.html

62. Ibid.

63. Matthews, C. (2009, January 5) Personal Communication. Chief Special Agent. BNSF Railway Police.

64. Operation Lifesaver (n.d.) Retrieved 2010, December 20, from http://www.oli.org/

65. Where the Road Meets the Rail. (n.d.) Retrieved 2010, December 20, from http://tti.tamu.edu/publications/researcher/newsletter.htm?vol=35&issue=2&article=1

66. Rail Security (n.d.) Securing our nation's rail systems. Retrieved 2010, December 20, from http://www.tsa.gov/what_we_do/rail/index.shtm

67. Where we Stand. (n.d.) Fact sheet. Retrieved 2010, December 20, from http://www.tsa.gov/press/where_we_stand/rail_security_facts.shtm

68. Ibid.

69. Ibid.

70. Matthews, C. (2009, January 5) Personal Communication. Chief Special Agent. BNSF Railway Police.

## Chapter 6

1. The History of Horse Racing. (n.d.) Retrieved 2010, December 20, from http://www.mrmike.com/explore/hrhist.htm

2. The Most Exciting Dogs in the World (n.d.) Greyhound Racing Association of America. Retrieved 2010, December 20, from http://www.gra-america.org/the_sport/history.html

3. Ibid.

4. Proverbs 30:29-31 (1990). *The Holy Bible: Containing the Old and New Testaments. King James Version.* A Regency Bible from Thomas Nelson Publishers

5. The Most Exciting Dogs in the World (n.d.) Greyhound Racing Association of America. Retrieved 2010, December 20, from http://www.gra-america.org/the_sport/history.html

6. Ibid.

7. Ibid.

8. Ibid.

9. Ibid.

10. Ibid.

11. Ibid.

12. Ibid.

13. Ibid.

14. Ibid.

15. Ibid.

16. The History of Horse Racing. (n.d.) Retrieved 2010, December 20, from http://www.mrmike.com/explore/hrhist.htm

17. Ibid.

18. Ibid.

19. Ibid.

20. Derby History (n.d.) 1874–1899 Kentucky and Louisville's early racing History. Retrieved 2010, December 20, from http://www.kentuckyderby.com/history/period/1874-1899

21. Ibid.

22. The History of Horse Racing. (n.d.) Retrieved 2010, December 20, from http://www.mrmike.com/explore/hrhist.htm

23. Ibid.

24. Ibid.

25. Reaves, B. A. (2007). *Census of State and Local Law Enforcement Agencies, 2004.* Washington D.C.: Bureau of Justice Statistics.

26. Williams, J. (2006, February 20) Personal Communication. Former Director of Enforcement, Texas Racing Commission.

27. The History of Horse Racing. (n.d.) Retrieved 2010, December 20, from http://www.mrmike.com/explore/hrhist.htm

28. Ibid.

29. Ibid.

30. Ibid.

31. Williams, J. (2006, February 20) Personal Communication. Former Director of Enforcement, Texas Racing Commission.

32. Texas Racing Commission (n.d.) Handbook of Texas Online. Retrieved 2010, December 20, from http://www.tshaonline.org/handbook/online/articles/TT/mdtnq.html

33. Texas Racing Act (1986) Retrieved 2010, December 20, from http://www.txrc.state.tx.us/laws/act/tratoc.php

34. Ibid.

35. Executive Division (n.d.) Texas Racing Commission. Structure of Agency. Retrieved 2010, December 20, from http://www.txrc.state.tx.us/agency/structure/exec_div.php

36. Ibid.

37. Ibid.

38. Ibid.

39. Ibid.

40. Williams, J. (2006, February 20) Personal Communication. Former Director of Enforcement, Texas Racing Commission.

# Endnotes

41. Texas Racing Commission: An Inventory of Records at the Texas State Archives, 1988–2000 (n.d.) Retrieved 2010, December 20, from http://www.lib.utexas.edu/taro/tslac/30044/30044-P.html

42. Williams, J. (2006, February 20) Personal Communication. Former Director of Enforcement, Texas Racing Commission.

43. Ibid.

44. Ibid.

45. Executive Division (n.d.) Texas Racing Commission. Structure of Agency. Retrieved 2010, December 20, from http://www.txrc.state.tx.us/agency/structure/exec_div.php

46. Williams, J. (2006, February 20) Personal Communication. Former Director of Enforcement, Texas Racing Commission.

47. Ibid.

48. Ibid.

49. Gougler, M. (2009, October 20) Personal Communication. Director of Enforcement, Texas Racing Commission.

50. Ibid.

51. Ibid.

52. Ibid.

53. Ibid.

54. Ibid.

55. Ibid.

56. Williams, J. (2006, February 20) Personal Communication. Former Director of Enforcement, Texas Racing Commission.

57. Ibid.

58. Ibid.

59. Gougler, M. (2009, October 20) Personal Communication. Director of Enforcement, Texas Racing Commission.

60. Williams, J. (2006, February 20) Personal Communication. Former Director of Enforcement, Texas Racing Commission.

61. Texas Racing Act (1986) Retrieved 2010, December 20, from http://www.txrc.state.tx.us/laws/act/tratoc.php

62. Gougler, M. (2009, October 20) Personal Communication. Director of Enforcement, Texas Racing Commission.

63. Ibid.

64. Williams, J. (2006, February 20) Personal Communication. Former Director of Enforcement, Texas Racing Commission.

## Chapter 7

1. Wolfenstine, M. R. (1970) *The manual of brands and marks*. Norman: University of Oklahoma Press.

2. Ibid.

3. Ibid.

4. Perkins, D., & Ward, N. (1984) *Brave men and cold steel: A history of range detectives and their peacemakers.* Fort Worth, TX: The Texas and Southwestern Cattle Raisers Association.

5. Ibid

6. Wolfenstine (1970). *The manual of brands and marks.*

7. Ibid.

8. Ibid.

9. Perkins & Ward (1984). *Brave men and cold steel.*

10. The Story of Our Efficient System of Brand Inspection. (n.d.) Retrieved 2010, December 20, from http://www.texascattleraisers.org/earlyDays/brand_inspection_tscra_Texas_cattle.asp

11. Perkins & Ward (1984). *Brave men and cold steel.*

12. Clarke, M. W. (1976) *A century of cow business: A history of the Texas and Southwestern Cattle Raisers Association.* Fort Worth, TX: The Texas and Southwestern Cattle Raisers Association.

13. Perkins & Ward (1984). *Brave men and cold steel.*

14. Ibid.

15. Ibid.

16. Ibid.

17. Clarke (1976). *A century of cow business.*

18. Ibid.

19. Ibid.

20. Ibid.

21. Ibid.

22. Perkins & Ward (1984). *Brave men and cold steel.*

23. The Story of Our Efficient System of Brand Inspection. (n.d.) Retrieved 2010, December 20 from http://www.texascattleraisers.org/earlyDays/brand_inspection_tscra_Texas_cattle.asp

24. Clarke (1976). *A century of cow business.*

25. Ibid.

26. Ibid.

27. Perkins & Ward (1984). *Brave men and cold steel.*

28. Ibid.

29. Ibid.

30. Clarke (1976). *A century of cow business.*

31. Gray, L. (2009, January 30) Personal Communication. Executive Director of Law Enforcement and Theft Prevention Services, Texas and Southwestern Cattle Raisers Association.

32. Ibid.

33. Ibid.

34. Ibid.

35. Ibid.

36. Ibid.

# Endnotes

37. Law Enforcement and Livestock Inspection (n.d.) TSCRA: Theft Protection. Retrieved 2010, December 20, from http://www.texascattleraisers.org/theftProtection.asp

38. Gray, L. (2009, January 30) Personal Communication. Executive Director of Law Enforcement and Theft Prevention Services, Texas and Southwestern Cattle Raisers Association.

39. Ibid.

40. Ibid.

41. Law Enforcement and Livestock Inspection (n.d.) TSCRA: Theft Protection. Retrieved 2010, December 20, from http://www.texascattleraisers.org/theftProtection.asp

42. The Story of Our Efficient System of Brand Inspection. (n.d.) Retrieved 2010, December 20, from http://www.texascattleraisers.org/earlyDays/brand_inspection_tscra_Texas_cattle.asp

43. Law Enforcement and Livestock Inspection (n.d.) TSCRA: Theft Protection. Retrieved 2010, December 20, from http://www.texascattleraisers.org/theftProtection.asp

44. Gray, L. (2009, January 30) Personal Communication. Executive Director of Law Enforcement and Theft Prevention Services, Texas and Southwestern Cattle Raisers Association.

45. Drovers News Source ( 2010, March 23) TSCRA special rangers recover millions in stolen livestock Retrieved 2010, December 20, from http://www.drovers.com/news_editorial.asp?pgID=675&ed_id=7082

46. Perkins & Ward (1984). *Brave men and cold steel.*

## Chapter 8

1. Reaves, B. A. (2007). *Census of State and Local Law Enforcement Agencies, 2004.* Washington D.C.: Bureau of Justice Statistics.

2. Collins, P. (1992) Big plan on campus. *Security Management.* V36 n3 p26.

3. Ibid.

4. Ibid.

5. History (n.d.) Retrieved 2010, December 20, from http://www.yale.edu/police/overview.html#History

6. Collins, P. (1992) Big plan on campus. *Security Management.* V36 n3 p26.

7. History (n.d.) Retrieved 2010, December 20, from http://www.yale.edu/police/overview.html#History

8. Ibid.

9. Ibid.

10. Collins, P. (1992) Big plan on campus. *Security Management.* V36 n3 p26.

11. Ibid.

12. Ibid.

13. Alderete, L. (2006, September 19) Personal Communication. Texas Commission on Law Enforcement Officer Standards and Education.

14. About UTPD (n.d.) Retrieved 2010, December 20, from http://www.utexas.edu/police/about/

15. Alderete, L. (2006, September 22) Personal Communication. Texas Commission on Law Enforcement Officer Standards and Education.

16. Gardner, R. (2006, September 22) Personal Communication. Texas Commission on Law Enforcement Officer Standards and Education.

17. Holbrooks, J. (2009, March 10). Personal Communication. Director of University Department of Public Safety, Sul Ross State University.

18. Ibid.

19. Ibid.

20. Ibid.

21. Campus Law Enforcement 2004-2005 (2008, February) U.S. Department of Justice, Office of Justice Programs, Bureau of Justice Statistics, Special Report Retrieved 2010, December 20, from http://www.ojp.usdoj.gov/bjs/pub/ascii/cle0405.txt

22. Siegel, D. (1994, May) What is behind the growth of violence on college campuses? The United States of violence: A special section – cover story. *USA Today*. Retrieved 2010, December 20, from http://findarticles.com/p/articles/mi_m1272/is_n2588_v122/ai_15282515/

23. Ibid.

24. Angelo State University: History and Traditions (n.d.) Retrieved 2010, December 20, from http://www.angelo.edu/history_and_traditions/index.html

25. Angelo State University: About ASU (n.d.) Retrieved 2010, December 20, from http://www.angelo.edu/asu_facts/

26. Ibid.

27. Adams, J (2008, December 12) Personal Communication. Director of Public Safety/Chief of University Police, Angelo State University

28. Ibid.

29. Ibid.

30. Ibid.

31. Ibid.

32. Ibid.

33. Ibid.

34. A History of Sul Ross (n.d.) Retrieved 2010, December 20, from http://www.sulross.edu/pages/3718.asp

35. Who was Sul Ross? (n.d.) Retrieved 2010, December 20, from http://www.sulross.edu/pages/3586.asp

36. A History of Sul Ross (n.d.) Retrieved 2010, December 20, from http://www.sulross.edu/pages/3718.asp

37. Quick Facts (n.d.) Retrieved 2010, December 20, from http://www.sulross.edu/pages/3030.asp

38. More About Sul Ross (n.d.) Retrieved 2010, December 20, from http://www.sulross.edu/pages/3489.asp

39. Holbrooks, J (2009, March 10). Personal Communication. Director of University Department of Public Safety, Sul Ross State University.

40. Adams, M. (1989, April 28). Past and present figures of Sul Ross State University Security and University Police – 1927–1989. Unpublished Research Paper.

41. Ibid.

42. Ibid.

43. Holbrooks, J. (2009, March 10). Personal Communication. Director of University Department of Public Safety, Sul Ross State University

44. Ibid.

45. Ibid.

46. Ibid.

47. Ibid.

48. Ibid.

49. Dahlstrom, R. (2009, June 8) Personal Communication. Chief, University of Texas at Austin.

50. Authority and Jurisdiction (n.d.) Retrieved 2010, December 20, from http://www.utexas.edu/police/about/authority.html

51. Dahlstrom, R. (2009, June 8) Personal Communication. Chief, University of Texas at Austin.

52. Ibid.

53. Ibid.

54. Holbrooks, J. (2009, June 10) Personal Communication. Director of University Department of Public Safety, Sul Ross State University

55. Dahlstrom, R. (2009, June 8) Personal Communication. Chief, University of Texas at Austin.

56. Ibid.

57. Ibid.

58. Questions raised about Virginia Tech security: Reporters, students, professors discuss if reaction could have been better (2007, April 17). Associated Press. Retrieved 2010, December 20, from http://www.msnbc.com/id/18142745

59. Fact File: Deadly College Shootings in US: Massacre at Virginia Tech (n.d.) Retrieved 2010, December 20, from http://www.msnbc.com/id/18137414/ns/us_news-crime_and_courts/

60. Ibid.

61. Dahlstrom, R. (2009, June 8) Personal Communication. Chief, University of Texas at Austin.

62. Plohetski, T., Wear, B., Kreytak, S., & George, P. (2010, September 29). UT gunman the only victim in morning of chaos: Police search Austin teen's home looking for clues into shooting. *American Statesman*. Retrieved 2010, December 20, from http://www.statesman.com/news/local/ut-gunman-the-only-victim-in-morning-of-chaos

63. Ibid.

64. Samano, C. (2008, November 25) College campus shootings increase desire for tighter security. Retrieved 2010, December 20, from http://media.www.paisanoonline.com/media/storage/paper975/news/2008/11/25/News/College.Campus.Shootings.Increase.Desire.For.Tighter.Security-3561757.shtml

65. Ibid.

66. Hunter, R. (2009, April 28) Personal Communication. Deputy, Brewster County Sheriff's Office.

67. Dahlstrom, R. (2009, June 8) Personal Communication. Chief, University of Texas at Austin.

68. History of the Jeanne Clery Disclosure of Campus Security Policy and Crimes Statistics Act. (n.d.) Retrieved 2010, December 20, from http://www.foundation.csus.edu/HR/csus_act.html

69. Ibid.

70. Ibid.

71. Siegel, D. (1994, May) What is behind the growth of violence on college campuses? The United States of violence: A special section – cover story. *USA Today*. Retrieved 2010, December 20, from http://findarticles.com/p/articles/mi_m1272/is_n2588_v122/ai_15282515/

## Chapter 9

1. Fire Marshal (n.d.) Retrieved 2010, December 20, from http://www.co.travis.tx.us/fire_marshal/default.asp

2. Index Crimes Law and Legal Definition. (n.d.) Retrieved 2010, December 20, from http://definitions.uslegal.com/i/index-crimes/

3. Arson is a Crime (n.d.) Retrieved 2010, December 20, from http://www.cityofandrews.org/marshal_files/page0005.htm

4. Kondratick, J (2009, January 22) Personal Communication. Fire/Arson Investigator, Texas State Fire Marshal's Office.

5. Reaves, B. A. (2007). *Census of State and Local Law Enforcement Agencies, 2004*. Washington D.C.: Bureau of Justice Statistics.

6. Kondratick, J. (2009, January 22) Personal Communication. Fire/Arson Investigator, Texas State Fire Marshal's Office.

7. History of the Texas State Fire Marshal's Office (n.d.) Retrieved 2010, December 20, from http://www.tdi.state.tx.us/fire/fmhistoy.html

8. Ibid.

9. Fire Marshal (n.d.) Retrieved 2010, December 20, from http://www.co.travis.tx.us/fire_marshal/default.asp

10. Fire Protection Sprinkler Law and Legal Definition (n.d.) Retrieved 2010, December 20, from http://definitions.uslegal.com/f/fire-protection-sprinkler/

11. Fire Safety Inspections (n.d.) Retrieved 2010, December 20, from http://www.tdi.state.tx.us/fire/fmfsi.html

12. Fort Bend County Department: Fire Marshal (2008, October 10) Retrieved 2010, December 20, from http://www.tcfp.state.tx.us/employment.asp

13. Basic Certification Requirements (n.d.) Retrieved 2010, December 20, from http://www.tcfp.state.tx.us/standards/basic_certification.asp

14. Ibid.

15. Kondratick, J. (2009, January 22) Personal Communication. Fire/Arson Investigator, Texas State Fire Marshal's Office.

16. Ibid.

17. Fire Marshal (n.d.) Retrieved 2010, December 20, from http://www.co.travis.tx.us/fire_marshal/default.asp

# Endnotes

18. Fire Marshal's Departmental Information (n.d.) Retrieved 2010, December 20, from http://www.cityofandrews.org/marshal_files/page0001.htm

19. Vardeman, D. (2009, March 3) Personal Communication. Fire Marshal, City of San Angelo.

20. Ibid.

21. Ibid.

22. Ibid.

23. Ibid.

24. Ibid.

25. Kondratick, J (2009, January 22) Personal Communication. Fire/Arson Investigator, Texas State Fire Marshal's Office.

26. Ibid.

27. Ibid.

28. Ibid.

29. Ibid.

30. Fire Safety Inspections (n.d.) Retrieved 2010, December 20, from http://www.tdi.state.tx.us/fire/fmfsi.html

31. State Fire Marshal's Office (n.d.) Retrieved 2010, December 20, from http://www.tdi.state.tx.us/fire/fire.html

32. Ibid.

33. Ibid.

34. Ibid.

35. Ibid.

36. Fire Marshal (n.d.) Retrieved 2010, December 20, from http://www.co.travis.tx.us/fire_marshal/default.asp

## Chapter 10

1. Mange, T. (2006, November 29) Personal Communication. Texas Department of Public Safety.

2. Wadman, R. C., & Allison, W. T. (2004) *To protect and to serve: A history of police in America*. Upper Saddle River, NJ: Pearson Prentice Hall.

3. Ibid.

4. Ibid.

5. Metz, L. C. (1979) *Dallas Stoudenmire: El Paso Marshal*. Norman: University of Oklahoma Press.

6. Ibid.

7. Ibid.

8. Ibid.

9. Ibid.

10. Ibid.

11. Ibid.

12. Train Robber Hanks Killed (1902, April 20) The New York Times Retrieved 2010,

December 20, from http://query.nytimes.com/mem/archive-free/pdf?_r=1&res=9D05E5D71 03DEE32A25753C2A9629C946397D6CF

13. Proceedings of the Thirty-sixth Annual Convention, City Marshals and Chiefs of Police Union of Texas (1934) Dallas, TX.

14. Proceedings of the Thirtieth Annual Convention, City Marshals and Chiefs of Police Union of Texas (1928) Houston, TX.

15. History of EPPD (n.d.) Retrieved 2010, December 20, from http://www/ci.el-paso.tx.us/police/history1.asp

16. Job: Deputy City Marshal (n.d.) Retrieved 2010, December 20, from http://www.fortworthgov.org/municipalcourt/default.aspx?id=58556

17. Ibid.

18. Marshal's Office (n.d.) Retrieved 2010, December 20, from http://www.baytown.org/government/courts/marshals-office.htm

19. New Marshal Unit to Track Outstanding Warrants (2007, January 30) Retrieved 2010, December 20, from http://www.sanantonio.gov/news/NewsReleases/nr07MarshalUnit.asp

20. Great Texas Warrant Roundup (2009, February 15). *San Angelo Standard Times.*

21. Ibid.

22. Gossett, L. (2009, April 27). Personal Communication. San Angelo Municipal Court.

23. Albertson, B. (2008, November 12). Personal Communication. Deputy City Marshal, San Angelo.

24. Nunez, J. (2009, February 26). Personal Communication. Deputy City Marshal, San Angelo.

25. Ibid.

26. Albertson, B. (2008, November 12) Personal Communication. Deputy City Marshal, San Angelo.

27. Ibid.

28. Ibid.

29. Nunez, J. (2009, February 26) Personal Communication. Deputy City Marshal, San Angelo.

30. Ibid.

31. Ibid.

32. Ibid.

33. New Marshal Unit to Track Outstanding Warrants (2007, January 30) Retrieved 2010, December 20, from http://www.sanantonio.gov/news/NewsReleases/nr07MarshalUnit.asp

34. Ibid.

35. Ibid.

## Chapter 11

1. Kerr, K. A. (1985). *Organized for Prohibition: A new history of the Anti-Saloon League.* New Haven, CT: Yale University Press.

2. McWilliams, P. (1996). Ain't nobody's business if you do. Part IV: Six chapters in search of a shorter book. Prohibition: A lesson in the futility (and danger) of prohibiting. Retrieved 2010, December 20, from http://www.mcwilliams.com/books/aint/402.htm

3. Reaves, B. A. (2007). *Census of State and Local Law Enforcement Agencies, 2004.* Washington D.C.: Bureau of Justice Statistics.

4. Lindsey, S. (2009, January 14) Personal Communication. Law Enforcement Agent, Texas Alcoholic Beverage Commission.

5. Fallen Angels (n.d.) Retrieve 2010, December 20, from http://www.tabc.state.tx.us/about_us/tribute_to_fallen_agents.asp

6. Ibid.

7. Lindsey, S., (2009, January 14) Personal Communication. Law Enforcement Agent, Texas Alcoholic Beverage Commission.

8. Ibid.

9. Ibid.

10. Ibid.

11. TABC Agents (n.d.) Retrieve 2010, December 20, from http://www.tabc.state.tx.us/enforcement/location_inspections.asp

12. Ibid.

13. Ibid.

14. Lindsey, S. (2009, January 14). Personal Communication. Law Enforcement Agent, Texas Alcoholic Beverage Commission.

15. TABC Commissions (2008, February 1) Texas Alcoholic Beverage Commission Enforcement Policy, Procedures and Forms Manual. Policy 10.00.0. Texas Alcoholic Beverage Commission.

16. Ibid.

17. Ibid.

18. Field Training Program (2008, February 1) Texas Alcoholic Beverage Commission Enforcement Policy, Procedures and Forms Manual. Policy 9.00.0. Texas Alcoholic Beverage Commission.

19. Lindsey, S. (2009, January 14) Personal Communication. Law Enforcement Agent, Texas Alcoholic Beverage Commission.

20. Ibid.

21. Ibid.

22. Ibid.

23. Lindsey, S. (2009, April 24). Personal Communication.

24. TABC Agents (n.d.) Retrieve 2010, December 20, from http://www.tabc.state.tx.us/enforcement/location_inspections.asp

25. Lindsey, S. (2009, April 24) Personal Communication.

26. Ibid.

27. Ibid.

28. Source Investigations (n.d.) Retrieve 2010, December 20, from http://www.tabc.state.tx.us/enforcement/source_investigations.asp

29. Lindsey, S. (2009, April 24) Personal Communication.

30. Minor Sting Operations (n.d.) Retrieve 2010, December 20, from http://www.tabc.state.tx.us/enforcement/minor_stings.asp

31. Ibid.

32. Cops in Shops (n.d.) Retrieve 2010, December 20, from http://www.tabc.state.tx.us/enforcement/cops_in_shops.asp

33. Operation Fake Out (n.d.) Retrieve 2010, December 20, from http://www.tabc.state.tx.us/enforcement/operation_fakeout.asp

34. Ibid.

35. Special Events (n.d.) Retrieve 2010, December 20, from http://www.tabc.state.tx.us/enforcement/special_events.asp

36. Lindsey, S. (2009, April 24). Personal Communication.

37. Lindsey, S. (2009, January 14). Personal Communication.

38. Reporting Alcohol-Related Violations/Filing a Complaint Against a TABC-Licensed Location (n.d.) Retrieve 2010, December 20, from http://www.tabc.state.tx.us/enforcement/complaint_about_a_location.asp

39. Texas Underage Drinking Hotline (n.d.) Retrieve 2010, December 20, from http://www.tabc.state.tx.us/enforcement/texas_underage_drinking_hotline.asp

40. TABC Agents (n.d.) Retrieve 2010, December 20, from http://www.tabc.state.tx.us/enforcement/location_inspections.asp

41. West, Matt (2009, March 5) Personal Communication. Former Law Enforcement Agent, Texas Alcoholic Beverage Commission.

42. Ibid.

43. Lindsey, S. (2009, January 14). Personal Communication.

44. Ibid.

45. Ibid.

46. Texas police look in bars for signs of drunkenness (2006, March 29). The Washington Times. Retrieved 2010, December 20, from http://www.washingtontimes.com/news/2006/mar/29/20060329-120349-2378r//

47. Parsons, J. (2006, April 14) TABC suspends Operation Last Call. *The Houstonist.* Retrieved 2010, December 20, from http://houstonist.com/2006/04/14/tabc_suspends_o.php

## Chapter 12

1. Bailiff. (n.d.) Retrieved 2010, December 20, from http://www.britannica.com/EBchecked/topic/49275/bailiff

2. Falcone, D. N. (2005) *Prentice Hall's dictionary of American criminal justice, criminology and criminal law.* Upper Saddle River, NJ: Prentice Hall.

3. Haskins, C. H. (1960). *Norman institutions.* New York: Frederick Ungar Publishing Co.

4. Falcone, D. N. (2005) *Prentice Hall's dictionary.*

5. Buffardi, H. C. (1998) The History of the Office of Sheriff: Chapter 5 Retrieved 2010, December 20, from http://www.correctionhistory.org/html/chronicl/sheriff/ch5.htm

6. Edward I: Statutes and Ordinances (nd) Retrieved 2010, December 20, from http://www.constitution.org/sech/sech_052.htm

7. Bailiff. (n.d.) Retrieved 2010, December 20, from http://www.britannica.com/EBchecked/topic/49275/bailiff

8. Horle, C. W. (1988). *The Quakers and the English legal system, 1660–1688.* Philadelphia: University of Pennsylvania Press.

# Endnotes

9. Ibid.

10. Bailiff. (n.d.) Retrieved 2010, December 20, from http://www.britannica.com/EBchecked/topic/49275/bailiff

11. Ibid.

12. Ibid.

13. Horle, C. W. (1988). *The Quakers and the English legal system, 1660–1688.*

14. Bailiff. (n.d.) Retrieved 2010, December 20, from http://www.britannica.com/EBchecked/topic/49275/bailiff

15. Ibid.

16. Schmalleger, F. (2007). *Criminal justice today: An introductory text for the 21st century.* (9th ed.) Upper Saddle River, NJ, Pearson, Prentice Hall.

17. Falcone, D. N. (2005) *Prentice Hall's dictionary.*

18. Programs—Bailiffs & Warrant Officers (n.d.) Retrieved 2010, December 20, from http://www.tmcec.com/tmcec/Programs/BailiffsandWarrantOfficers

19. Jennings, T. (2009, February 26) Personal Communication. Bailiff, Tom Green County Court.

20. Gaines, L. H., & Miller, R. L. (2009). *Criminal justice in action* (5th ed.) Belmont, CA: Thompson Wadsworth.

21. Ibid.

22. Little Known Facts about the Court Security and Transportation Division. (n.d.) Retrieved 2010, December 20, from http://www.co.bexar.tx.us/BCsheriff/courtfacts.htm

23. Jennings, T. (2009, February 26). Personal Communication.

24. Ibid.

25. Ibid.

26. Ibid.

27. Ibid.

28. Ibid.

29. Ibid.

30. Ibid.

31. Ibid.

32. Little Known Facts about the Court Security and Transportation Division. (n.d.) Retrieved 2010, December 20, from http://www.co.bexar.tx.us/BCsheriff/courtfacts.htm

33. BCSO Court Security History (n.d.) Retrieved 2010, December 20, from http://www.co.bexar.tx.us/BCsheriff/courthistory.htm

34. Ibid.

35. BCSO Court Security Staff (n.d.) Retrieved 2010, December 20, from http://www.co.bexar.tx.us/BCsheriff/courtstaff.htm

36. BCSO Court Security and Transport (n.d.) Retrieved 2010, December 20, from http://www.co.bexar.tx.us/BCsheriff/courtsecurity.htm

37. Ibid.

38. BCSO Court Security Satellite Booking (n.d.) Retrieved 2010, December 20, from http://www.co.bexar.tx.us/BCsheriff/satellite.htm

## Chapter 13

1. Game Warden Cadet Job Posting (2009, February 2) Retrieved 2010, December 20, from http://www.tpwd.state.tx.us/business/jobs/postings/game_warden_cadet/

2. Sigler, W. F. (1972). *Wildlife Law Enforcement.* (2nd ed) Dubuque, IA: William C. Brown Company Publishers.

3. Ibid.

4. Ibid.

5. Ibid.

6. Ibid.

7. Ibid.

8. Ibid.

9. Ibid.

10. Reaves, B. A. (2007). *Census of State and Local Law Enforcement Agencies, 2004.* Washington D.C.: Bureau of Justice Statistics.

11. Aguilar, C. (2009, February 12) Personal Communication. Game Warden, Texas Parks and Wildlife Department.

12. TPWD Activities and History. (n.d.) Retrieved 2010, December 20, from http://www.tpwd.state.tx.us/business/about/history/

13. Ibid.

14. Game Warden Memorial. (n.d.) Retrieved 2010, December 20, from http://www.tpwd.state.tx.us/warden/memorial/

15. TPWD Activities and History. (n.d.) Retrieved 2010, December 20, from http://www.tpwd.state.tx.us/business/about/history/

16. Aguilar, C. (2009, February 12). Personal Communication. Game Warden, Texas Parks and Wildlife Department.

17. Ibid.

18. Ibid.

19. Game Warden Cadet Job Posting (2009, February 2) Retrieved 2010, December 20, from http://www.tpwd.state.tx.us/business/jobs/postings/game_warden_cadet/

20. Ibid.

21. Ibid.

22. Ibid.

23. Aguilar, C. (2009, February 12). Personal Communication. Game Warden, Texas Parks and Wildlife Department.

24. Ibid.

25. Ibid.

26. Ibid.

27. Ibid.

28. Ibid.

29. Operation Game Thief (n.d.) Retrieved 2010, December 20, from http://www.tpwd.state.tx.us/warden/ogt/

Endnotes 173

30. Outdoor Learning. (n.d.) Retrieved 2010, December 20, from http://www.tpwd.state.tx.us/learning/

31. Ibid.

32. Ibid.

33. Ibid.

## Chapter 14

1. Biddle, S. (2009, June 19). Personal Communication. Investigator Sergeant, Brazos County Attorney's Office.

2. Willis, W. (2009, February 10). Personal Communication. Former Polk County District Attorney Investigator.

3. County Attorney (n.d.) Retrieved 2010, December 20, from http://www.dallam.org/county/atty.shtml

4. Alderete, Lillian. (2006, September 22). Personal Communication. Texas Commission on Law Enforcement Officer Standards and Education.

5. Career and Employment Opportunities—Investigator (n.d.) Retrieved 2010, December 20, from http://app.dao.hctx.net/Careers/Investigator.aspx

6. Employment Requirements (n.d.) Retrieved 2010, December 20, from http://dentoncounty.com/dept/main.asp?Dept=23&link=263

7. About TDCAA (n.d.) Retrieved 2010, December 20, from http://www.tdcaa.com/about

8. Ibid.

9. Career and Employment Opportunities—Investigator (n.d.) Retrieved 2010, December 20, from http://app.dao.hctx.net/Careers/Investigator.aspx

10. Hightower, M. (2007, May 2) Investigators Forum Posting. Retrieved 2010, December 20, from http://tdcaa.infopop.net/2/OpenTopic?a=tpc&s=347098965&f=5340985611&m=5331050941

11. Willis, W. (2009, February 10) Personal Communication. Former Polk County District Attorney Investigator.

12. Webb, B. (2009, February 13) Personal Communication. Former District Attorney Investigator.

13. Willis, W. (2009, February 10) Personal Communication. Former Polk County District Attorney Investigator.

14. Lyons, J. (2007, May 4) Investigators Forum Posting. Retrieved 2010, December 20, from http://tdcaa.infopop.net/2/OpenTopic?a=tpc&s=347098965&f=5340985611&m=7371020941

15. Willis, W. (2009, February 10). Personal Communication. Former Polk County District Attorney Investigator.

16. Ibid.

17. Ibid.

18. Ibid.

19. Ibid.

20. Ibid.

21. Ibid.

22. Ibid.

23. Ibid.

24. Englert, M. (2009, April 23). Personal Communication. Tom Green County Attorney Investigator.

25. Ibid.

26. Ibid.

27. Ibid.

28. Ibid.

29. Ibid.

30. Harris County Attorney (n.d.) Retrieved 2010, December 20, from http://www.co.harris.tx.us/coatty/

31. Biddle, S. (2009, June 19). Personal Communication. Investigator Sergeant, Brazos County Attorney's Office.

32. Ibid.

33. Ibid.

34. Hinojosa, M. (2009, August 7). Personal Communication. Investigator, Denton County District Attorney's Office.

# Bibliography

Adams, M. (1989, April 28). Past and present figures of Sul Ross State University Security and University Police—1927-1989. Unpublished Research Paper.

Anderson, D. C. (1995). *Crime and the politics of hysteria: How the Willie Horton story changed American justice.* New York: Times Books, Random House.

Babbie, E. R. (2006). *The practice of social research.* (11th ed.). Belmont, CA: Wadsworth.

Baker, T. (1966). *The Normans.* New York: The MacMillan Company.

Butler-Kay, K., & Graham, J. (2000). *Criminal justice in Texas.* Boston: Allyn and Bacon.

Clarke, M. W. (1976). *A century of cow business: A history of the Texas and Southwestern Cattle Raisers Association.* Fort Worth, TX: The Texas and Southwestern Cattle Raisers Association.

Collins, P. (1992). Big plan on campus. *Security Management.* V36 n3 p26.

Constitution of the State of Texas (2006). All references to the Texas Constitution are as it appeared on August 1, 2006. Available at http://tlo2.tlc.state.tx.us/txconst/toc.html.

del Carmen, R. V. (2007). *Criminal Procedure.* Belmont, CA: Thomson-Wadsworth.

Dempsey, J. S. & Forst, L. S. (2005). *An introduction to policing.* (3rd ed.). Belmont CA: Wadsworth.

Dewhurst, H. S. (1955). *The railroad police.* Springfield, IL: Thomas Books.

Falcone, D. N. (2005). *Prentice Hall's dictionary of American criminal justice, criminology and criminal law.* Upper Saddle River, NJ: Prentice Hall.

Field Training Program (2008, February 1) Texas Alcoholic Beverage Commission Enforcement Policy, Procedures and Forms Manual. Policy 9.00.0. Texas Alcoholic Beverage Commission.

Gaines, L. H., & Miller, R. L. (2009). *Criminal justice in action* (5th ed.). Belmont, CA: Thompson Wadsworth.

Great Texas Warrant Roundup. (2009, February 15) *San Angelo Standard Times.*

Hardin, John Wesley. (n.d.). Retrieved 2010, December 20, from Handbook of Texas Online.

Haskins, C. H. (1960). *Norman institutions.* New York: Frederick Ungar Publishing Co.

Hatley, A. G. (1999). *Texas constables: A frontier heritage.* Lubbock: Texas Tech University Press.

*Holt v. State,* 887 S.W.2d. 16 (TexCrim.App. 1994).

Holtz, L. E., & Spencer, W. J. (2004). *Texas contemporary criminal procedure.* Longwood, FL: Gould.

Horle, C. W. (1988). *The Quakers and the English legal system, 1660–1688.* Philadelphia: University of Pennsylvania Press.

Horton, D. M., & Turner, R. K. (1999). *Lone star justice: A comprehensive overview of the Texas criminal justice system.* Austin, TX: Eakin Press.

Kanovitz, J., & Kanovitz, M. (2005). *Constitutional Law* (10th ed.). New York: Matthew Bender and Co.

Kerr, K. A. (1985). *Organized for Prohibition: A new history of the Anti-Saloon League.* New Haven, CT: Yale University Press.

LaFave, Wayne R. (2003). *Criminal Law* (4th ed.). St. Paul: Thomson-West.

LexisNexis (2007). Texas Criminal and Traffic Law Manual. Charlottesville, VA: LexisNexis, pp. ix-xvi, LH1-LH6; Steven Edmonds. (2005). 2005-2007 Legislative Update. Austin: Texas District and County Attorneys Association.

*McMillan v. State,* 609 S.W.2d. 784 (Tex.Crim.App. 1980).

Meeker, J. (2007–2008). Arrest, search and seizure without a warrant manual, p. 63; LexisNexis, Texas Criminal Law and Traffic Manual, ed. Charlottesville, VA: LexisNexis.

Meeker, J. (2005). Arrest, search and seizure without a warrant manual. Pflugerville, TX: CLEAR.

Meeker, J. (2003). Search warrant manual. Pflugerville, TX: CLEAR. LexisNexis. Texas Criminal Law and Traffic Law Manual. Charlottesville, VA. LexisNexis, 2007, pp. LG-47–48.

Metz, L. C. (1979). *Dallas Stoudenmire: El Paso Marshal.* Norman: University of Oklahoma Press.

*Michigan Dept. of State Police v. Sitz,* 496 U.S. 444 (1990)

*Miranda v. Arizona,* 384 U.S. 436, 1966.

Nichols, L. D., Robbins, R. K., & Harrelson, D. B. (2004). *The Texas Peace Officer* (9th ed.). vols. 1 and 2. Richmond CA: McCutcheon.

———. (2006). *The Texas Peace Officer* (10th ed.). Richmond CA: McCutcheon.

Pelz, B., & Pelz, T. (2001). *Introduction to criminal justice: Texas edition.* Belmont, CA: Wadsworth.

Perkins, D., & Ward, N. (1984). *Brave men and cold steel: A history of range detectives and their peacemakers.* Fort Worth, TX: The Texas and Southwestern Cattle Raisers Association.

Proceedings of the Thirtieth Annual Convention, City Marshals and Chiefs of Police Union of Texas (1928) Houston, TX.

Proceedings of the Thirty-sixth Annual Convention, City Marshals and Chiefs of Police Union of Texas (1934) Dallas, TX.

Proverbs 30:29–31 (1990). *The Holy Bible: Containing the Old and New Testaments. King James Version.* A Regency Bible from Thomas Nelson Publishers.

Public Law 106-110 (Nov 24, 1999) 106th Congress.

Reamey, G. S., & Harkins, D. J. (1988). Texas Jurisprudence 3rd, "Police, Constables and Sheriff"; Texas Code of Criminal Procedure, Article 14.03 (d), (g), "Warrantless Arrest Jurisdiction in Texas."

Reamey, G. S., & Harkins, J. D. (1988). Warrantless arrest jurisdiction in Texas: An analysis and proposal. *Saint Mary's Law Journal*, 19 (1988).

Reaves, B. A. (2007). *Census of state and local law enforcement agencies, 2004.* Washington D.C.: Bureau of Justice Statistics.

Richardson, J. F. (1975). The early years of the New York Police Department. In J. Skolnick & T. Gray (Eds.), *Police in America.* Boston: Little, Brown.

Roth, M. P. (2005). *Crime and punishment: A history of the criminal justice system.* Belmont, CA: Wadsworth.

Rotunda, R., & Nowak, J. (1999). *Treatise on Constitutional Law*, vol. 1. St. Paul, MN: West Group.

Schmalleger, F. (2007). *Criminal justice today: An introductory text for the 21st century.* (9th ed.). Upper Saddle River, NJ: Pearson, Prentice Hall.

Sigler, W. F. (1972). *Wildlife law enforcement* (2nd ed). Dubuque, IA: William C. Brown Company Publishers.

Stover, J. F. (1961). *American railroads.* Chicago: University of Chicago Press.

TABC Commissions. (2008, February 1). Texas Alcoholic Beverage Commission Enforcement Policy, Procedures and Forms Manual. Policy 10.00.0.

Texas Jurisprudence 3rd. (2006). Vol. 59, Police Constables and Sheriffs. San Francisco: Bancroft Whitney.

Wadman, R. C., & Allison, W. T. (2004). *To protect and to serve: A history of police in America*. Upper Saddle River, NJ: Pearson Prentice Hall.

Walker, S. (1983). *The police in America: An introduction*. New York: McGraw Hill.

Williams, J. H. (1988). *A great and shining road: The epic story of the transcontinental railroad*. New York: Times Books.

Wolfenstine, M. R. (1970). *The manual of brands and marks*. Norman: University of Oklahoma Press.

## Personal Communications:

Adamcik, Ben. Constable, Precinct 3, Dallas County, Texas. Oct. 26, 2007.

Adams, J. Director of Public Safety/Chief of University Police, Angelo State University. Dec. 12, 2008.

Aguilar, C. Game Warden, Texas Parks and Wildlife Department. Feb. 12, 2009.

Albertson, B. Deputy City Marshal, San Angelo. Nov. 12, 2008.

Alderete, L. Texas Commission on Law Enforcement Officer Standards and Education. Sept. 19 and Sept. 22, 2006.

Biddle, S. Investigator Sergeant, Brazos County Attorney's Office. June 19, 2009.

Block, L. Texas Department of Public Safety. Feb. 24, 2009.

Brewer, Mark. Constable, Precinct 1, Wichita County, Texas. Dec. 17, 2007 and Jan. 7, 2008.

Cobb, Joan. Deputy Constable, Precinct 4, Tom Green County. August 12, 2007.

Dahlstrom, R. Chief, University of Texas at Austin. June 8, 2009.

Englert, M. Tom Green County Attorney Investigator. April 23, 2009.

Gardner, R. Texas Commission on Law Enforcement Officer Standards and Education. Sept. 22, 2006.

Gossett, L. San Angelo Municipal Court. April 27, 2009.

Gougler, M. Director of Enforcement, Texas Racing Commission. Oct. 20, 2009.

Gray, L. Executive Director of Law Enforcement and Theft Prevention Services, Texas and Southwestern Cattle Raisers Association. Jan. 30, 2009.

Green, D. Senior Special Agent. Union Pacific Railroad Police. Feb. 20, 2009.

Hester, A. Constable, Precinct 4, Tom Green County. October 20, 2007.

Hinojosa, M. Investigator, Denton County District Attorney's Office. August 7, 2009.
Holbrooks, J. Director of University Department of Public Safety, Sul Ross State University. March 10 and June 10, 2009.
Holbrooks, J. W. Constable, Precinct 2, Crosby County, TX. Jan. 10, 2008.
Hunter, R. Deputy, Brewster County Sheriff's Office. April 28, 2009.
Jaurez, A. Constable, Precinct 4, Webb County, Texas. October 30, 2007.
Jennings, T. Bailiff, Tom Green County Court. Feb. 26, 2009.
Koca, J. Criminal Justice Director, Concho Valley Council of Governments. Jan. 2, 2006.
Kondratick, J. Fire/Arson Investigator, Texas State Fire Marshal's Office. Jan. 22, 2009.
Lindsey, S. Law Enforcement Agent, Texas Alcoholic Beverage Commission. January 14, and April 24, 2009.
Macias, M. Law Enforcement Academy, Sul Ross State University. Nov. 29, 2010.
Mange, T. Texas Department of Public Safety. Nov. 29, 2006.
Mares, L. Special Agent in Charge, BNSF Railway Police. Feb. 10, 2009.
Martinez, S. Payroll Clerk, Webb County, Texas. Dec. 17, 2007.
Matthews, C. Chief Special Agent, BNSF Railway Police. Jan. 5, 2009.
Nunez, J. Deputy City Marshal, San Angelo. Feb. 26, 2009.
Recruiting Office. Dallas Police Department. Sept. 7, 2010.
Webb, B. Former District Attorney Investigator. Feb. 13, 2009.
West, M. Former Law Enforcement Agent, Texas Alcoholic Beverage Commission. March 5, 2009.
Williams, J. Former Director of Enforcement, Texas Racing Commission. Feb. 20, 2006.
Willis, W. Former Polk County District Attorney Investigator. Feb. 10, 2009.
Vardeman, D. Fire Marshal, City of San Angelo. March 3, 2009.

# Index

9-11 (Sept. 11, 2001, terrorist attacks), 99, 100, 117, 118, 136, 146

## A

Adamcik, Ben, 40, 156, 178

Adams, James, 85, 86, 164, 175, 178

Adult Protective Services, 145

Aguilar, Cynde, 130, 133, 172, 178

Albertson, Brian, 102, 107, 108, 168, 178

Alderete, Lillian , 6, 32, 140, 150, 154, 163, 164, 173, 178

Alley, Thomas V., 31

American Jockey Club, 61, 62

Amtrak, 47, 49, 51, 56, 156

Angelo State University, 85, 86, 164, 178

Aristides (horse), 62

arrest, 4, 16, 20–22, 24–26, 31–33, 35, 37, 52, 81, 87, 98, 100, 103, 105, 107, 109, 112, 116, 117, 119, 120, 127, 136, 143, 145, 152, 176

    warrantless arrest, 20, 23, 26, 152, 177

arson, 4, 8, 95–101, 166, 167, 179

Anti-arson Act, 95

Awareness Week, 100

Austin, Texas, 43, 89, 116

Austin, John, 31

Austin, Stephen F., 3, 31

Automatic Fire Sprinkler Law, 96

## B

background check, 12, 13, 50, 66, 67, 76, 84, 106, 114, 119, 134

Bailiff, 8, 108, 122–129, 170, 171, 179

    bailiwick, 123

    duties of, 126–129

    first appointed, 125

    qualifications, 126

    special requirements, 126

Barber, John Phillip, 49

Battle of Little Big Horn, 60

Bennett, Thomas Henry, 49

Bexar County, 128, 129

Bible, 59, 159, 177

Biddle, Scott, 145, 173, 174, 178

Big Spring, Texas, 43

Index                                                                                       181

Bill Blackwood Law Enforcement Management Institute of Texas (LEMIT), 44, 156

Black Death, 30

Blue Skin Club, 82

Boating While Intoxicated, 136

bootlegging, 118
  still(s), 110, 118

Boston, Massachusetts, 103

Brand Registry, 71, 72

Brazos County, 140, 145

Brewer, Mark, 38, 155, 156, 178

Brown, Mike, 127

Buffalo Soldiers, 137

Bureau of Justice Statistics, 49

Burlington Northern Santa Fe Railway (BNSF), 47, 49, 52–55

Burn Awareness Week, 101

## C

calls for service, 37, 52, 100

Cattle Brand Inspectors, 6, 7, 71–73, 75–78
  duties, 74–78
  first appointed, 72, 73
  killed, 75
  qualifications, 76
  special requirements, 76

cattle theft, 72, 74, 75

Certification, Peace Officer, 15, 16, 21, 33, 54, 84, 97, 140, 143, 147, 151, 166

Child Protective Services, 145

children, 43, 99–101
  missing and abused, 21, 22, 55

chivalry, 29, 30

Churchill Downs, 61

cities in Texas
  Big Spring, 43
  Dallas, 6, 13, 40, 49, 65, 116, 157
  El Paso, 32, 43, 54, 104, 105, 134
  Fort Worth, 6, 73, 74, 76, 77, 106, 157
  Hamilton, 135
  Houston, 2, 3, 116
  San Angelo, 43, 85, 94, 98, 99, 101, 102, 107, 108, 115, 117, 144
  San Antonio, 43, 74, 105, 107, 108

City Attorney, 99

City Manager, 99

City Marshal, 8, 102–109, 168, 177
  and Chiefs of Police Union, 105
  duties, 106–109
  first appointed, 104
  killed, 105
  qualifications, 106
  special requirements, 106

Civil War, 32, 127

Clements, William P., 142

Clery Act, 91, 92

Clery, Jeanne, 91, 166

Colt's Manufacturing Company, 78

Concho County, 41

confessions, 24

Constable, 1–3, 5–7, 18, 19, 28–38, 40–44, 82, 106, 109, 123, 124, 143, 147, 153–155, 177

    Deputy, 32, 34, 41–43, 143

    duties, 34–41

        Mental Health, 42–44

    first appointed, 31

    killed, 31

    Leadership Development Training, 44

    Lord High Constable, 30

    qualifications, 33, 34

    special requirements, 34

    removal of, 35, 36

Continuing Education, 11, 15, 34, 44, 126

contraband, 23, 52, 65, 66

Cops in Shops, 116, 117, 170

counties of Texas

    Bexar, 128, 129

    Brazos, 140, 145

    Concho, 41

    Crosby, 2, 36, 38, 40, 41

    Dallas, 36, 40, 41

    Gonzales, 72

    Harris, 140, 141, 145, 174

    Harrison, 118

    Johnson, 142

    Laredo, 41

    Polk, 140, 142, 143

    Sterling, 41

    Tom Green, 28, 41–43, 122, 127, 138, 144

    Travis, 98

    Webb, 41

    Wichita, 36, 38, 40, 41, 155

County

    Commissioners Court, 33–35, 127

    Court, 30, 124, 127, 128

    Jail, 5, 41, 43, 104, 105, 107, 117, 119, 127–129, 148, 150

    Judge, 8, 25, 42, 107, 108, 124–129

County Attorney Investigators, 139, 140, 142, 144

    duties, 142, 144–146

    first appointed, 139, 140

    qualifications, 140, 141

    special requirements, 141, 142

coursing, 60

Court Reporter, 125

# Index

Court Security and Transport Division, 128

Crews, Joseph Thomas, 112

Crosby County, 2, 36, 38, 40, 41

Crossing Accident Reduction Enforcement (CARE), 52

Custer, George Armstrong, 60

## D

Dahlstrom, Robert, 89–91, 165, 166, 178

Dallas, Texas, 6, 13, 40, 49, 65, 116, 157

Dallas County, 36, 40, 41

Death Investigators, 139, 146

Defense Attorney, 125

Diaz, Larry, 46

District Attorney, 9, 139, 140, 142, 146, 147

    Prosecutor, 9, 64, 74, 125, 140, 141

District Attorney Investigators, 9, 140, 142, 143

    duties, 142–144

    first appointed, 139, 140

    qualifications, 140, 141

    special requirements, 141, 142

Donnelly, Jim, 82

drug(s), 2–4, 12, 14, 23, 24, 65, 68, 84, 106, 127, 134

    testing, 12, 14, 50, 63–67, 106

DWI checkpoints, 26, 116

## E

Egypt/Egyptian, 59, 71

El Paso, Texas, 32, 43, 54, 104, 105, 134

elections, 5, 30, 32–34, 140

eligibility standards, 11

Emperor Theodosius, 29

England, 29, 30, 60, 61, 81, 123

Englert, Mickey, 138, 144, 174, 178

ethics, 21, 126

exclusionary rule, 24

## F

family violence, 12, 15, 22

    domestic violence, 37, 134, 141, 144

Federal Bureau of Investigation (FBI), 4, 51, 89

federalism, 17

Field Training Officer, 42, 52

Fire

    Department Emergency Board, 96

    Extinguisher Law, 96

    fighter, 101

    Marshal, 8, 88, 94–101, 166, 167

        duties, 98–101

        first appointed, 96

qualifications, 97

special requirements, 97, 98

State Fire Marshal's Office, 96, 97, 99–101

Prevention Week, 99, 101

Safety Inspection Services, 96, 97

fireworks, 96

Flammable Liquids Law, 96

forfeiture, 16, 23, 24

Fort Worth, Texas, 6, 73, 74, 76, 77, 106, 157

fraud, 95, 98

# G

Garrett, William W., 49

Game Warden, 8, 37, 88, 130–137, 172

duties, 135–137

first appointed, 132, 133

killed, 133

qualifications, 134

special requirements, 135

Training Academy, 135

Gonzales County, 72

Gougler, Mike, 66–68, 161, 178

Grade Crossing Collision Investigation (GCCI), 52

Graham, Larry, 87

grand jury, 98, 101, 142–144

Gray, Larry, 70, 76, 77, 162, 163, 178

Greyhound Racing Association, 61

Great Texas Warrant Roundup, 107, 168, 176

Green, David, 54

Green, Thomas, 127

Green Living, 137

# H

Hamilton, Texas, 135

Hardin, John Wesley, 32, 154, 176

Harris County, 140, 141, 145, 174

Harrison County, 118

hate crimes, 22

Hayes, Walter P., 87

Haz-mat, 52

Hester, Alvie, 28, 41, 155, 156, 179

Holbrooks, Johnnie, 46, 87, 88, 164, 165, 179

Holbrooks, J. W., 36–38, 149, 155, 179

Homeland Security, 2, 5, 52, 56, 57, 69, 119, 127, 131, 133, 135, 137, 144, 148, 156

Houston, Texas, 2, 3, 116

hurricanes, 52, 54, 133, 136, 147

Ike, 115, 120, 133

Rita, 133

# Index

## I

Indian Territory, 73, 132

inspection(s), 56, 64, 71, 74, 75, 77, 87, 88, 96, 97, 112, 113, 115, 116, 136, 162, 163, 166, 167

International Association of Chiefs of Police, 21

Interstate Commerce Commission, 73

## J

Jennings, Tonia, 122, 127, 171, 179

Jockey Club, 61

    American, 61, 62

Johnson County, 142

Joint Terrorism Task Force, 89

Johnson, William, 104

Juarez, Augustine, 41

jurisdiction, 4–7, 17–20, 22, 26, 32, 35, 36, 50, 51, 64, 68, 76, 83, 98, 101, 108, 109, 113, 123–126, 140, 142, 143, 165

jury, 34, 124, 126, 142, 144

Justice of the Peace, 32, 34, 35, 38

Justices of the Peace and Constables Day, 44

juvenile(s), 24, 26, 43, 108, 119

## K

K-9, 52–54, 56, 96

Keith, Don E., 142

Kentucky Derby, 61, 62

King, 29, 30, 59, 60, 124, 125, 131

King Alfred, 29

King Tutankhamen, 59

King, Rodney, 2

King, Stephen, 30

Koca, Jim, 42, 156, 179

Kondratick, John, 99, 166, 167, 179

## L

Lake Amistad, 134

Laredo County, 41

law enforcement, 1–9, 11–13, 15, 16, 18, 21, 22, 25, 29, 30–33, 37, 38, 40–44, 49, 50–55, 62, 68, 69, 75–77, 81, 83, 85, 90, 91, 95, 97, 98, 100, 101, 103–107, 109, 111, 112, 115, 116, 119, 120, 125, 129, 131, 133, 136, 137, 143, 146–148, 163, 164

    academies, 13, 150

    federal, 1, 4, 5, 75, 77

    local, 42, 56, 68, 75, 87–89, 107, 143, 144

    state, 5, 75, 77

Lewis, Oliver, 62

licensing, 8, 12, 13, 21, 33, 62, 63, 66, 67, 96, 101, 106, 112, 140

Lindsey, Shuddell, 115, 116, 169, 170, 179

## M

Magna Carta, 30

Mares, Luis, 54, 157–159, 179

Masterson, Bat, 48

Matthews, Charles, 53, 54, 57, 157–159, 179

Meincke, Bill, 65, 66

mentally ill, 40, 42–44

*Michigan Department of State Police v. Sitz*, 26, 153, 176

*Miranda v. Arizona*, 24, 152, 176

Moose Warden, 132

Mothers Against Drunk Driving (MADD), 111

Munn, Charles A., 60

## N

National Incident Management System (NIMS), 91

natural disasters, 52

response to, 131, 133

New Haven Police Department, 82

Norman Conquest, 30

North Texas State Hospital, 39

Nunez, Johanna, 108, 168, 179

## O

Oller, Pierre, 62

Operation Fake Out, 116, 117, 119, 170

Operation Game Thief, 136, 172

Operation Last Call, 119

Operation Lifesaver, 55, 159

Oxford University, 81

## P

Panhandle and Southwestern Stockman's Association, 73

pari-mutuel betting, 61, 62

gambling, 4, 59, 61, 62, 115, 120

peace officer, 6, 7, 9, 11–13, 15–26, 32–35, 37, 44, 50, 64, 65, 71, 77, 84, 96, 97, 99, 101, 113, 114, 123, 126, 127, 133–135, 139, 140, 142–145, 147, 148, 150, 151

mental health officer, 16, 42–44

Pearson, Delbert H., 112

Peeler, Tom, 75

Pennsylvania Railroad Police Act, 48

Personal Recognizance Bond Satellite Booking Office, 128

Pinkerton, Allan, 48

Pinkerton Detective Agency, 48

Plymouth Colony, 30

police chief, 85, 103–105, 109

police power, 17, 18, 48, 114, 125

Polk County, 140, 142, 143

Pollard, Benjamin, 103

polygraph, 14, 66

Postin, Timothy, 87
precinct, 32–36, 38, 40–42
Prohibition, 82, 111, 112
Protective Services
    Adult, 145
    Child, 145
public education, 52, 55, 56, 100, 101, 115, 117, 131, 135–137
public law 106–110, 51, 158, 177

## Q

Queens
    Anne, 61
    Cleopatra, 59
    Hatshepsut, 59

## R

racial profiling, 16, 20
racing, 59, 61–69, 159, 160
    Greyhound, 59–61, 63, 67
    Quarter horse, 62
    Thoroughbred, 60–62
Racing Commission investigator, 3, 7, 64, 67, 68
    duties, 65–68
    first appointed, 63
    qualifications, 64
    special requirements, 65
racetrack(s), 61, 64, 67, 68
    Churchill Downs, 61
    G. Rollie White Downs, 64
    Hilaleah Racetrack, 60
railroad police, 3, 7, 19, 47–57, 157, 158
    duties, 52–56
    first appointed, 48
    killed, 49
    qualifications, 50
    special provisions, 51
Raymond, Harry, 133
Reno Brothers, 47
riots, 23, 82
Roman Empire, 29
Ross, Lawrence Sullivan, 86

## S

San Angelo, Texas, 43, 85, 94, 98, 99, 101, 102, 107, 108, 115, 117, 144
San Antonio, Texas, 43, 74, 105, 107, 108
search and seizure, 16, 24
    stop and frisk, 25
search warrants, 25
Secretary of Agriculture, 74
Seguin, Juan, 31
Selman, John, 32
September 11 (9-11), 52, 53, 57, 89, 119, 144

sheriff, 1, 3, 5–7, 9, 18–20, 30–33, 36, 37, 39, 41, 42, 77, 86, 98, 100, 108, 123–128, 144

Simpson, OJ, 2

Smith, Owen Patrick, 60

Smoke Detectors in Hotels Law, 96

source investigations, 116, 169

Special Rangers, 26, 75–77

Special Weapons and Tactics (SWAT), 52, 128

Statute of Westminster, 30

Statute of Winchester, 124

Sterling County, 41

sting operations, 8, 116, 169

Stock Raisers Association of Northwest Texas, 72, 73

Stoudenmire, Dallas, 104, 105

Stud Book

American, 61

general, 61

subpoena, 34, 98, 101, 143

Sul Ross State University, 13, 80, 86, 87, 89, 164

summoning assistance, 20

# T

Take Me Fishing Program, 136, 137

Tays, John B., 104

Texas Alcoholic Beverage Code, 23, 117

Texas Alcoholic Beverage Commission, 5, 8, 23, 83, 111, 112, 118, 119

duties, 112–115, 119

first appointed, 112

killed, 112

qualifications, 114

special requirements, 114, 115

Texas and Southwestern Cattle Raisers Association, 26, 72, 74–76

Texas Code of Criminal Procedure, 19–26, 32, 152

Texas Commission on Fire Protection, 97

certifications, 97

Texas Commission on Law Enforcement Officer Standards and Education (TCLEOSE), 6, 11–13, 15, 16, 21, 33, 41, 42, 97, 114, 126

Texas Constitution, 3, 7, 17, 18, 25, 31, 32, 175

Article 1, 18, 24

Article 5, 18, 34, 151, 155

Bill of Rights, 3, 18

Texas Department of Insurance, 88, 96

Texas Department of Parks and Wildlife, 130, 132, 133, 135, 147

divisions, 133

Texas Department of Public Safety, 2–6, 25, 35, 50, 66, 76, 115, 150

Texas District and County Attorneys Association, 141

Texas Education Code, 19, 151

Texas Family Code, 22, 24, 152

Texas Fire Escape Law, 96

Texas Fish and Oyster Commission, 132, 133

Texas Game and Fish Commission, 133

Texas Government Code, 18, 19, 33, 151

Texas Legislature, 11, 18, 20, 26, 33, 44, 64, 96

Texas Local Government Code, 19, 151

Texas Municipal Courts Education Center, 126

Texas Occupations Code, 12

Texas Parks and Wildlife Code, 133

Texas Racing Act, 63, 65, 68, 160, 161

Texas Racing Commission, 2, 3, 7, 19, 59, 62–65, 67, 68, 147, 161

Texas Railroad Association, 50

Texas Rangers, 3, 5, 7, 19, 73, 86, 104

Texas Senate Bill 15, 63

Texas Senate Bill 162, 87

Texas State Bar Association, 140

Texas State Parks Board, 133

Texas State Senate, 44

Texas Transportation Code, 23

threats, 22, 89, 91, 92, 101, 128, 129, 145

Title 49 USC 207.5, 50, 51, 157, 158

Tom Green County, 28, 41–43, 122, 127, 138, 144

Tooley, Colton, 90

Torres, M. V., 49

Track Stewards, 64–66

traffic enforcement, 5, 23, 40, 41, 87, 115, 147

train robbery, 47, 52, 105, 157

Travis County, 98

## U

Uniform Crime Reports, 4, 87, 95, 149

    Index Crime, 4, 95, 166

Union Pacific Railroad, 52, 54

United States Border Patrol, 5, 119

United States Constitution, 17, 18, 21, 25, 151

    Bill of Rights, 18

    Eighteenth Amendment, 111

    Fourth Amendment, 24–26

    Tenth Amendment, 17, 151

    Twenty-first Amendment, 111

United States Marshals Service, 125

University Police, 6–8, 81–85, 87, 89–92

    campus police, 6, 8, 81–92

duties, 83–90
first appointed, 81–83
qualifications, 84
special requirements, 84
University of Texas (UT), 83, 89

**V**

Vardeman, Don, 94, 99, 167, 179
Venango County, PA, 31
Virginia Tech, 8, 90, 92, 165

**W**

Waterloo Cup Meet, 60
Webb County, 41
West, Matthew, 110, 118, 170, 179
White River Lake, 36–38
Whitman, Charles, 90
Wichita County, 36, 38, 40, 41, 155
Williams, Joe, 133
Williams, John T, 65, 66, 149, 160, 161, 179
Williamson, Ansel, 62
Willis, W. D., 143, 144, 173, 179
wiretapping, 25
Wiser, Bill, 82
World War II, 82

**Y**

Yale University, 81, 82, 87
Yellowstone National Park, 132
Young, Charles, 87

www.ingramcontent.com/pod-product-compliance
Lightning Source LLC
Chambersburg PA
CBHW030321080526
44584CB00012B/652